Red I

Blue 1

Bottom

CW00706464

RED LINE

How Push Came to Shove

BLUE LINE

Between the National Hockey League

BOTTOM LINE

and its Players

Marc Edge

New Star Books | VANCOUVER | 2004

New Star Books Ltd.
107 – 3477 Commercial Street
Vancouver, BC   V5N 4E8
www.NewStarBooks.com

Publication of this work is made possible by grants from the
Canada Council, the British Columbia Arts Council, and the
Department of Canadian Heritage Book Publishing Industry
Development Program.

 Conseil des Arts
du Canada   Canada Council
for the Arts   Canada   BRITISH
COLUMBIA
ARTS COUNCIL

Printed on 100% post-consumer recycled paper
and bound in Canada by Imprimerie Gauvin.
First printing, September 2004

LIBRARY AND ARCHIVES CANADA CATALOGUING IN PUBLICATION

Edge, Marc, 1954 –

  Red line, blue line, bottom line : how push came to shove
between the National Hockey League and its players / Marc
Edge.

ISBN 1-55420-011-3

  1. Hockey players — Salaries, etc. 2. Hockey players —
labor unions. 3. National Hockey League — Finance. I. Title.

GV847.4.E33 2004   331'.041796962   C2004-905186-5

Contents

Preface

It starts with a fight for control of the play. One player pins the other up against the boards for a little longer than is strictly necessary; the answering face wash seems a bit gratuitous, too. Before long the players are trading trash talk, pushing and shoving. Then the inevitable staredown, and when neither side blinks, the gloves come off.

But this time there's no referee or linesman to break things up. For this brawl is taking place not on the ice, but at the bargaining table; not between hockey tough guys, but between union and management tough guys. On one side is the National Hockey League itself, claiming that it is fighting for its very survival. On the other, the NHL Players' Association, a ninety-eight-pound weakling no more after years of being pushed around by the owners. At stake is a new collective bargaining agreement — which governs all NHL player contracts, including rules relating to free agency — to replace the one that took a half-season play stoppage in 1994-95 to achieve.

Now many are starting to wonder not when, but even *if* the NHL will settle its differences with its players and unlock the turnstiles at its rinks around North America. Players are making alternate plans to play overseas in

Europe — and not just European-born players. New leagues are being planned, and if they can make it off the ground and fly for even a short while, they may get a lift to lofty altitudes with an influx of big-name players if the NHL cancels its 2004-05 season entirely for lack of a new collective agreement with the NHLPA. Whether the two sides could negotiate an agreement in time for the start of the following season would then become a question on which the fate of the National Hockey League might hinge. If it's not possible, the NHL as we know it might quickly become redundant.

Maybe they're bluffing, but the last time this scrap took place, ten years ago, the two sides went to the very brink, holding out well into January before reaching a compromise agreement right at the league-imposed deadline for salvaging the 1994-95 season. As a result, an abbreviated forty-eight-game schedule was played instead of the usual eighty-two games, and the Stanley Cup playoffs followed as they always do. This time team owners are threatening to go all the way and use the ultimate weapon in their arsenal in an attempt to get players to give in. Canceling the 2004-05 NHL season would wipe out the Stanley Cup playoffs for the first time in more than a century. It would be the first time since 1893 that the oldest championship trophy competed for in North American professional sports was not awarded at least once in a year. But some hockey historians point out that Lord Stanley's mug is a challenge trophy that does not rightfully belong to the National Hockey League, which merely appropriated it in a power grab during the first half of the twentieth century. If the NHL doesn't want to play for hockey's ultimate prize, perhaps someone else should be allowed to.

Team owners are crying poverty and insisting that

players agree to a "salary cap," such as exists in various forms in the three other major professional sports leagues in North America, to save them from their own free-spending ways. They have trotted out some high-priced financial experts in the form of Arthur Levitt and his crew of accountants to attest to the fact that the league as a whole did indeed lose a total of $273 million in 2002-03 as claimed. They also certify that nineteen of the thirty NHL franchises are losing money because of high player salaries that eat up three-quarters of all league revenues, which would be the highest percentage in professional sports — if the owners aren't fudging the figures. The owners have given NHL commissioner Gary Bettman extraordinary powers and a mandate to bring "cost certainty" to the league and some sanity to its economics. Bettman is the father of the salary cap, having introduced the concept to the National Basketball Association in the early 1980s when he was an executive in that league. He was hired in 1992 to bring one to the NHL, but failed to do so in 1994, settling instead for a salary cap on rookies only, which did little to keep salaries from climbing. This time, Bettman is serious about settling for nothing less than tying salaries firmly to revenues in order to ensure that owners can't lose money, even if they try.

For their part, the players are skeptical about the claims of poverty made by owners, pointing to their lack of honesty in the past and to the well-documented accounting tricks that team owners in other sports leagues have used to fiddle the books to make it look like they're losing money when they're not. They'd like to have a close look at the league's finances for themselves, rather than taking someone else's word for the fact owners are losing money by the bushel. The players like the free-market system just the way it is because it allows team owners and general managers eager to get their hands on Stanley's cup to spend freely on free agents. As a result, player salaries in the NHL have more than tripled in the past decade to an average of $1.79 million a year, which is still less than the $2.5 million that the average Major League Baseball player makes, which in turn is dwarfed by the staggering $4.9-million average salary in the NBA. Besides, NHL players point out, nobody is holding a gun to the head of NHL team owners and forcing them to sign high-priced contracts for free agents. They think that the system of free enterprise is working just fine, thank you, and that if NHL teams couldn't afford to pay such high salaries, they simply wouldn't offer them.

At the same time, the players realize that they've got it good — better than hockey players have ever had it, if salaries are any indication. They have a vested interest in keeping the golden goose alive and thriving. They realize that NHL owners' ability to pay has been stretched to its limit — and perhaps beyond — by the peculiar economics of the league. The NHLPA has even offered financial concessions in the form of a 5 percent salary rollback if team owners will agree to share some of their own revenues among themselves in an attempt to make NHL economics more cooperative and less cutthroat. That's not enough for Bettman and the NHL owners, however, who are insisting on a radical restructuring of the league's compensation system. "Whether we're going to blow it up and start over is really the union's call," Bettman said in 2003. Will Gary Bettman and the NHL push players to the brink, and perhaps push the game of hockey over it?

Caught in the middle, of course, is the long-suffering fan, who has not only had to pay ever-higher ticket prices to watch increasingly talent-diluted hockey teams, but now will have to go without hockey altogether. It's impossible to know how long it will take for the players and owners to settle their economic differences or, more importantly, how many hockey fans will still care when and if they do.

How did it ever get to this? Who's right? Who's wrong? Who is fudging the facts to their advantage in the public relations war of words? Will hockey survive this economic upheaval? By examining the issues in depth, by looking at what's happened in the past, and by comparing the experience of other sports leagues in dealing with these same recurring issues, *Red Line, Blue Line, Bottom Line* will, I hope, help the average fan gain greater insight into just what is going on behind closed doors in the hockey talks.

I think I now understand the old story about the artist who, when asked how long it took to finish her latest painting, answered: "My whole life." That's the way I feel after putting the finishing brushstrokes on this book, because it really does connect several fields of endeavor in which I have been engrossed over the past three decades or so. As a student of business and labor relations in the 1970s and '80s, I became fascinated by the dynamics of collective bargaining. I took my master's degree in labor and industrial relations at Michigan State University in 1982, where I also played a bit of hockey. (I'm always careful to assert quite truthfully that "I played hockey at Michigan State" and not "for Michigan State" — it was intramural only.) As a union member, I contributed what I could during one year on the executive and bargaining committees of The Newspaper Guild local in Vancouver. I'm sure it's just a coincidence that we ended up going on strike for seven weeks that spring of 1984. As a hockey writer more than two decades back, I was always more interested in the business aspects of the game than the on-ice escapades.

As an NFL season ticket holder throughout the 1980s, I suffered with every other football fan through in-season strikes twice — once for two months in 1982, and again in 1987 when we were "treated" to the spectacle of games played with "replacement" players for several weeks. No, I didn't use my tickets for those games. As a legal journalist for a decade until 1993, I think I gained enough understanding of the law to be able to explain complex "legalese" in lay terms. More recently, my study of journalism and mass communication at the doctoral level has helped illuminate for me some of the dynamics of persuasion and public opinion that will also be of interest in the current case study. But throughout, it has been my interest in hockey that has provided the common thread around which this book has been woven.

My career as a hockey writer was short-lived, spanning only a few years in the late 1970s and early 1980s until the magazine I wrote for went out of business. Nonetheless the experience provided much of the foundation upon which this book has been written. My first brief article for *Hockey* magazine, which was based in Connecticut and billed itself as "The Quality Hockey Magazine," was a bulletin on the new designer garb the Vancouver Canucks would sport starting with the 1978-79 season. The "designer" of the garish black-and-yellow uniforms was a San Francisco-based consultant who decided the colors would prove more aggressive on the ice than the team's previous colors of blue and green. At the suggestion of editor Keith Bellows, whom I had met through an acquaintance in Montreal, I became the magazine's western correspondent, based first in Calgary, where I worked in the business section of the *Calgary Herald,* then in Vancouver, where I resumed working for the *Province,* on which I had cut my teeth a few years earlier as a student sports writer. Over the next several years I filed features on such subjects as controversial junior hockey coach Ernie "Punch" McLean, hyperactive Canucks goalie Glen Hanlon, and the Atlanta Flames' move to Calgary. Soon I was informed by Bellows that I had been elevated to the lofty status of Contributing Writer, and that my name would be included on the masthead of every issue, whether I had contributed to it or not. My most embarrassing moment was during a 1979 interview, when I laughed out loud at Edmonton Oilers owner Peter Pocklington's prediction that his new NHL team would win the Stanley Cup within five years. I have to admit I was wrong to dismiss so lightly his collection of WHA refugees, who proved Peter Puck's prediction prescient right on schedule.

My lone cover story for *Hockey* magazine was on a young Los Angeles Kings winger who had recently graduated college only to find himself suddenly installed on the hottest line in hockey, alongside superstar Marcel Dionne. My admiration for Dave Taylor only grew when he started stuttering uncontrollably during our interview, and I recalled his embarrassing intermission appearance on the nationally televised *Hockey Night in Canada* the previous season as a rookie, when he had suffered a similar episode. Out of compassion, I decided to leave the stuttering angle out of my story and I advised my editor accordingly, only to read the information reinserted into the final published version. Speech therapy over the years helped rid Taylor of his stuttering affliction, and I was impressed that he played for seventeen stellar seasons before retiring as a grizzled veteran. An extremely well-paid veteran, I might add, as I had not realized until doing research for this book that he was actually the NHL's highest-paid player for several years after signing a multi-year contract in 1981 — the year after my cover story appeared. I'm sure that glowing publicity couldn't have had anything to do with such good financial fortune. Nahhhh . . .

My most memorable interview, however, was conducted in Calgary with Mervyn "Red" Dutton, then ninety years old, who had been an NHL player in the 1920s, later owned the New York Americans, and even briefly served as NHL president after Frank Calder's death in 1943. Dutton's tales of how he was cheated out of an NHL franchise and a lease of Madison Square Garden in favor of the cross-town Rangers stuck with me, as did his vow never to set foot in an NHL arena again, even if the league did come to his home town. I recall chuckling at my own naiveté, a few months later when the Calgary Flames played their first home game, and the puck was dropped for the ceremonial faceoff by none other than Red Dutton. My, how things can change when hockey is the game.

In some ways this book had its genesis in a road trip I went on during my brief career as a hockey writer, which involved taking the ferry from Vancouver to Victoria in 1980 to write a feature on top NHL prospect Dave Babych, who was then playing for the junior Portland Winterhawks. Fellow journalist and hockey-playing buddy Rolf Maurer came along for the ride. Rolf and I played hockey together for several years in the NHL — he as an ankle-skating forward and I as an unnaturally holy goalie. Not in the National Hockey League, mind you, but in the Nightside Hockey League, in which journalists from the *Vancouver Sun* and *Province* engaged about equally in puck chasing and beer drinking at Kitsilano ice rink every week at an ungodly early — or, depending on which shift you worked, late — hour. I always envied Rolf for having not only his own hockey card — designed courtesy of artist friend Linda Chobotuck — but also his own nickname inscribed on it: "Le Petit Dindon" (The Little Turkey).

Dave Babych didn't suit up for the game in Victoria that Rolf and I went to watch him play, but he did sit with us in a small scouting box overlooking the ice and chat throughout the three periods, which formed the basis of my article, along with other interviews. I can't remember exactly what the three of us discussed in such a leisurely fashion, but I think it was the insight both Rolf and I gained into the hockey business as a result that planted the seed in our minds that grew into this book almost a quarter of a century later. Dave Babych didn't do too badly for himself either, playing in the NHL even longer than Dave Taylor did — nineteen seasons — and growing a mustache almost as large as Lanny McDonald's in the process.

Rolf went into the book-publishing business shortly thereafter, and over the years we tossed around the idea of me writing a hockey book for him, but the occasion never presented itself as clearly as it has over the past year or so, with the labor showdown between the NHL and its players looming so largely. It is to Rolf that I owe the greatest debt of gratitude for being able to tell this tale. Stan Persky apparently deserves the credit for coming up with the title, which I am told has been kicked around — or perhaps more appropriately slapped around — the offices of New Star Books for several years now. (I must, however, claim inspiration for the clever subtitle myself.) As she did for my first book, *Pacific Press: The Unauthorized Story of Vancouver's Newspaper Monopoly* (Vancouver: New Star Books, 2001), Audrey McClellan again deserves a purple heart for serving as my editor. Through the miracle of the Internet and e-mail she has, perhaps fortunately for her, managed to perform the exercise both times without our ever actually meeting in person. One of these days, Audrey, we simply must get together. Simon Fraser University librarian Mark Bodnar was of great assistance in helping me navigate the dungeons and dragons that make up the Lexis-Nexis online database, and Tyler Currie of the NHLPA did what he could to help steer me in the right direction as well. Of course, any factual blunders and logical tautologies that follow are entirely my own damned fault.

Red Line

Blue Line

Bottom Line

CHAPTER 1

Hockey Night in Ornskoldsvik

ANNOUNCER: Forsberg passes to Sakic . . . right in front to Naslund . . . He scores! And MoDo has won the 2005 Stanley Cup!

Couldn't happen? Think again. If push comes to shove for any length of time in the labor dispute between the National Hockey League and the NHL Player's Association, some of the league's best players — and hockey's most coveted trophy — could be migrating to Europe for a season or two, even permanently. The Stanley Cup, after all, is a challenge trophy that in its early days was played for by teams from different leagues in different countries. The NHL may have appropriated Lord Stanley's mug for the past half century or so, but if it's not going to award it in 2005, perhaps someone else should.

In the looming New World Order in hockey, a small town near the Arctic Circle in Sweden could soon become the new center of global dominance. Forget Detroit, a.k.a. Hockeytown, U.S.A. Forget Toronto, a.k.a. Hockeytown, Canada. Ornskoldsvik is Hockeytown, Sweden. Soon it could be Hockeytown, Europe. With a population of only 56,000, this small fishing village and mill town on the Baltic coast has nonetheless produced some of the best players in the NHL, including Peter Forsberg, Markus Naslund, and the Sedin twins, Daniel and Henrik. A frigid 350 miles north of Stockholm, Ornskoldsvik is known for two exports — pickled herring and hockey players. The MoDo pulp and paper company has long sponsored the town's hockey team, which began play in the 1930s. Over the past thirty years the MoDo team has been demoted from Sweden's Elite League to the First Division only once — in 1984, the last time the team was rebuilding after being drained of its top players. At that time, MoDo alumni Tomas Gradin, Lars Lindgren, and Lars Molin left to help the Vancouver Canucks advance to the 1982 Stanley Cup finals.

In the mid-1990s, national and local hero Peter Forsberg — who was immortalized on a Swedish postage stamp depicting his gold-medal winning goal in the 1994 Olympics — jumped to the bright lights and big salaries of the National Hockey League. Forsberg helped the Colorado Avalanche to a pair of Stanley Cup victories and along the way helped himself to an eight-figure salary. Naslund, who has been one of the top NHL snipers for years, was joined in Vancouver by the Sedin twins in 2000 in hopes of finally bringing hockey's Holy Grail to the Canucks. When Daniel and Henrik Sedin were drafted second and third overall in 1999, they became the highest Swedish picks ever in the NHL's amateur draft. But if play in North America's top league is halted for any length of time, all of the above could be returning to star for their hometown team. And they could take some of their new-found friends from North America with them.

Forsberg, who has been bothered by persistent injuries, has long been rumored to be considering a return to European play as an alternative to the harsh physical grind of the NHL. He owns a skate-sharpening business in Ornskoldsvik, and in 2003 he opened a golf course there. After signing a one-year $11-million contract with Colorado in 2003, Forsberg told the Swedish newspaper *Aftonbladet* that his return to MoDo "can't be that far away."[1] His father Kent, who last coached MoDo a decade ago, will return as the team's bench boss for the 2004-05 season. Already the Ornskoldsvik team is set in goal with the return of Tommy Salo from his extended tour of duty in the NHL with the Islanders, Oilers, and Avalanche. As well, some of the top young Swedish players are choosing to sign with teams in their homeland rather than the NHL in anticipation of a lockout. Alexander Steen, the 2002 first-round draft choice of the Toronto Maple Leafs, whose father Tomas was a long-time NHLer with the old Winnipeg Jets, signed with MoDo after he was reportedly "aggressively recruited" by Kent Forsberg — possibly with the promise of playing alongside his son Peter.[2]

HOCKEY'S COMING UPHEAVAL

The European vacation that the world's best hockey will be going on starting in the fall of 2004 might turn into an extended relocation if the league locks out its players for any length of time in its desperate bid to wrest back the advantage it held for so many years in labor negotiations. And if the NHL doesn't win the fight it has picked with its players' association quickly — and the players promise that won't happen — the shift in hockey supremacy

1. Kevin Paul Dupont, "Teams Spending Time Correcting Market," *Boston Globe,* July 6, 2003, p. C11.
2. Ken Campbell, "Leaf prospect pulls a rare Swedish switch," *Toronto Star,* June 17, 2004, p. E8.

could become permanent. A new rival league — the reborn World Hockey Association — is also setting up North American operations, albeit somewhat tentatively and to much skepticism. The NHL's demand for a salary cap — or other form of "cost certainty" designed to save team owners from their own free-spending ways — could result in a fight to the finish. When the dust clears after a season or two has been missed, there might not even be an NHL anymore.

There has been a transformation of NHL economics going on for more than a decade now, and this shifting of the tectonic plates is about to rock the hockey landscape with a jolt of earthquake proportions. The future direction of the sport may have as much to do with the rising geopolitical fortunes of Europe, compared to North America, as with the fractured labor economics of the NHL. The bargaining-table advantage in negotiations, so long held by NHL owners, has for the past decade or so increasingly been enjoyed by players, who have walked away with wildly escalating salaries at contract time as a result. As they try to regain their dominance over players, NHL owners might be willing to kill the golden goose that enriched them for decades, or at least watch as it takes flight across the Atlantic to Europe. If that happens, they will have nothing but their own greed to blame.

In their eagerness to rake in hundreds of million of dollars in expansion fees over the past decade, NHL owners have not once but twice extended the hard-won collective bargaining agreement that they locked players out for half of the 1994-95 season to get, assuming that it was better to renew the deal than to allow the threat of labor unrest to lower the price potential owners were willing to pay for an NHL franchise. When the 1995 deal was reached, pundits declared that victory in the labor dispute had clearly gone to the owners, but time has just as clearly proven that verdict hopelessly misguided. Without a salary cap to save free-spending owners from themselves, more and more players have emerged from salary negotiations as multi-millionaires. Owners thought the restrictions placed on free agency in the current collective agreement were sufficient to prevent that by keeping down the salaries paid to veteran players at one end of the seniority scale, and to rookies at the other.

The deal stipulated that veterans would not be eligible for unrestricted free agency until age thirty-two for the first three years of the deal, and thirty-one thereafter, not at age twenty-seven or twenty-eight as the players wanted. But as long-time baseball union head Marvin Miller observed in his memoirs, player salaries increase not from free agency itself, but due to the most basic of economic laws — supply and demand. Bidding wars for available players would only take place, Miller realized, by keeping the number of free agents low, "so that every year there would be, say, three or four players available at a particular position and many teams to compete for their services."[3]

At the other end of the age scale, a salary cap on rookies was the ultimate deal maker in 1995, a compromise accepted by owners in hopes of keeping entry-level salaries low. But again the joke was on NHL teams, as it took only a few years for player agents to find loopholes in the collective agreement language and continue to extract multi-million-dollar contracts from eager general managers.

The shameless money grab that was expansion of the

3. Marvin Miller, *A Whole Different Ball Game: The Sport and Business of Baseball* (Secaucus, NJ: Carol, 1991), p. 320.

NHL during the 1990s — from twenty-one teams in 1993 to thirty by 1999 — has not only caused the demand for players to go up, but also raised their salaries along with it. As Miller noted, this is a result of the most basic economic law — supply and demand — but there is little else that is basic about the economics of the National Hockey League. The "ego economics" of the league are predicated more on greed and one-upmanship than on fiscal responsibility or even balancing the books. As a result, team owners squandered most of their expansion gold on contracts for scarce free agents, bidding their salaries up wildly in the hope of profiting even more at playoff time — on and off the ice. Now that they finally realize the grim reality of what they agreed to, the owners want to change the rules of the game — again.

But increasingly the swift skaters who came to stock the expansion teams placed by the NHL brain trust in such hockey hotbeds as Atlanta, Georgia, and Columbus, Ohio, hailed not from Canada, which had traditionally been the prime breeding ground for hockey talent, or from the U.S., which has provided some of the game's brightest stars. More and more the rosters of the over-expanded and talent-diluted NHL were populated by Europeans, who found a lucrative market for their services. Now that the NHL game is going on hold — for how long, nobody knows — they're going home, and they're taking our game with them.

THE EAGLE HAS LANDED IN JAIL

This book is an attempt to better understand what is at the root of the labor dispute between the National Hockey League and its players' association, and thus perhaps to realize where it is taking the sport of hockey. It uses both theory — economic theory, labor relations theory, public relations theory, etc. — and more common-sense wisdom, such as Marvin Miller dispensed in his memoirs. For example, pendulum theory states that first things swing one way, then they swing the other. In common-sense terms, "What goes around, comes around."

The single most undeniable fact in the tenuous relations between the NHL and its players is that there has been a fundamental shift in them since Bob Goodenow took over as executive director of the NHL Players' Association in 1991. It is important to note that Goodenow is not so much the cause of this change in relations, as he is a result of them. Under the long rule of the disgraced Alan Eagleson, the NHLPA was pliable to the point of being putty in the hands of owners. That's because "the Eagle" had his hand in the pockets of both the players and the owners, profiting richly from the international hockey tournaments he was able to organize by playing both sides of the table masterfully. Under Eagleson's leadership, the NHL Players' Association was nothing more than a "company union" for twenty-five years, content to scramble for whatever crumbs team owners cared to throw it. Now that the players have the upper hand, they aren't about to give it up easily. What goes around, comes around.

It was only when the original World Hockey Association started operations in 1972 and provided some competition to the NHL that hockey salaries blipped upward. For a brief time in the 1970s, freedom of movement meant that puck chasers weren't the lowest-paid of professional athletes, as they always had been in the four major leagues in North America. For a while they earned more than players in the National Football League and even Major League Baseball. After the WHA ended with a whimper in 1979 and its four healthiest teams were folded into the NHL — in exchange for paying a handsome "expansion" fee each, of course — that all changed. Hockey players' salaries sank during the 1980s to again rank as the lowest in pro sports. By 1990, the average NHL salary was half of what it was in any of the other leagues.

NHL players began to point their fingers at Eagleson. Since they saw him packed off to jail, hockey players have again enjoyed increased salaries, under Goodenow's guidance, and now rank third among the four major leagues — ahead of NFL players — earning an average of $1.79 million annually. To believe that they would go back to the way things were without a fight to the finish is to ignore how badly they were exploited for so many years.

The litany of sins committed by R. Alan Eagleson while he was executive director of the NHL Players' Association will not be recounted here. For only a few of his misdeeds he was sentenced to eighteen months in prison (where he spent only six months before being released on parole) and ordered to pay $1 million in restitution to the former NHL players he systematically bilked for years.

The case against the Eagle was prosecuted to no small extent by retired NHLers such as the late Carl Brewer, who sniffed out the con job behind their paltry pensions. But the perilous process of bringing to light the misdeeds of the most powerful man in hockey was undertaken by some investigative journalists whose published work reads like a criminal indictment. Sports reporter Russ Conway of the Lawrence *Eagle-Tribune* in suburban Boston first published many of the scoops that led to Eagleson's arrest, and his investigative journalism got him short-listed for a 1992 Pulitzer prize. His 1995 book, *Game Misconduct: Alan Eagleson and the Corruption of Hockey,* is a case study well worth reading for any hockey fan — or journalism student. Bruce Dowbiggin, then a CBC television reporter, also did much of the investigative work on the Eagleson story, sometimes in collaboration with Conway.

Another comprehensive account of Eagleson's malfeasance — and that of the National Hockey League itself — was published in 1991 by the husband-and-wife writing team of David Cruise and Alison Griffiths as *Net Worth: Exploding the Myths of Pro Hockey.* Their exhaustive examination of the minutiae of deception that went on in NHL backrooms for decades led them to the following conclusion: "Hockey owners have always been as flint-edged and parsimonious a group as exists in professional sports."[4] The pension fund fiasco cooked up between Eagleson and the NHL — for which both parties escaped facing a multi-million-dollar lawsuit filed by retired players in 1998 only due to a legal technicality — was, according to the *Net Worth* authors, "the biggest sucker play in the history of professional sports."[5] For decades, in successive collective bargaining agreements, NHL players gave up the opportunity for increased free agency in exchange for supposed improvements to their pension plan. But, as Cruise and Griffiths chronicled, the money that team owners agreed to put into the pension fund came mostly from an accumulated surplus that rightfully belonged to the players anyway.

For years, NHL owners cried poverty and implored players to settle for less "for the good of the game." Even

4. David Cruise and Alison Griffiths, *Net Worth: Exploding the Myths of Pro Hockey* (Toronto: Penguin, 1991), p. 256.
5. Ibid., p. 266.

as recently as negotiations for the 1986 collective agreement, when the NHL was experiencing unprecedented prosperity with surging attendance and increased television revenues, they claimed that higher salaries brought by free agency would bankrupt many teams. Again the players bought it because it was sold to them by Eagleson. Again they settled for supposed improvements to their pension fund instead of the free agency that would bring them higher salaries. Again, as Cruise and Griffiths detail, "it was just one more con job pulled on the players by the owners."[6] That's why the showdown between the NHL and its players promises to be the mother of all sports shutdowns. That's why the sport of ice hockey may be going on a European holiday for a season or two — or even longer — and maybe taking the Stanley Cup with it.

UNLOCKING HOCKEY'S RICHES

Ironically, it was one of the NHL owners who started the tectonic plates of hockey shifting. Then Bob Goodenow got into the act, and the aftershocks have been reshaping the NHL landscape ever since. Even as the player revolt against Eagleson was brewing in the late 1980s, maverick owner Bruce McNall saw the big-time potential of hockey and decided to make a huge investment in the game's biggest star. Not only did the new Los Angeles Kings owner buy Wayne Gretzky from Edmonton Oilers owner Peter Pocklington for $18 million in 1988 — with a few players and draft choices thrown in to make it look like a trade — but he then did something unprecedented in league history. He voluntarily gave him a huge pay

6. Ibid., p. 298.

raise, doubling his annual salary to $2.5 million. In fact, McNall wanted to pay Gretzky even more. According to Cruise and Griffiths he offered him $3 million a year, but the modest Gretzky followed the lead of his idol, Gordie Howe, by insisting on taking less.[7]

For most of the 1980s, until Gretzky moved to L.A., Kings winger Dave Taylor was the league's highest-paid player. Not Gretzky, not Mario Lemieux, but the work-manlike former college player who just happened to land a spot on hockey's top line early in his NHL career. Play-ing alongside Hall of Fame center Marcel Dionne helped rank Taylor among the league's scoring leaders for sev-eral years, and he made the most of it — on and off the ice. Smart as a whip, Taylor parlayed his great good for-tune into the richest NHL contract signed to that date, extracting $6 million from former Kings owner Jerry Buss over seven years starting in 1981. Before 1990, much secrecy surrounded NHL salaries, but word of Tay-lor's unprecedented deal got out, and according to Dow-biggin in his book *Money Players: How Hockey's Greatest Stars Beat the NHL at Its Own Game,* "agents seeking information grabbed it like a drowning man grabs a life preserver."[8] Because salaries were not publicized, by agreement between the NHL and the players' association, many assumed that Gretzky was the game's highest-paid player, but according to Dowbiggin, "The Great One" admitted in 1984 that he didn't earn half of what Taylor was making.[9] Together, Gretzky and Taylor took the

7. Ibid., p. 333.

8. Bruce Dowbiggin, *Money Players: How Hockey's Greatest Stars Beat the NHL at Its Own Game* (Toronto: McClelland & Stewart, 2003), p. 113.

9. Ibid., p. 219.

Kings to the Stanley Cup finals in 1993, but they lost to the Montreal Canadiens. Taylor's playing career spanned seventeen seasons, after which he almost immediately took over duties as the team's general manager due to his sterling hockey acumen.

Soon NHL players realized that making their salaries public would help them negotiate better contracts with team owners, despite Eagleson's insistence that it wouldn't. Starting in 1990, salary disclosure became a major bargaining lever with which agents were able to ratchet up the pay scale in pro hockey. That was the next tectonic shift. Salary disclosure, along with arbitration, which had existed for years but had been ineffective in the absence of disclosure, proved to be powerful weapons that enabled players to finally get salaries that approached market value. Before long a frantic game of salary leapfrog was on. Gretzky's big-money contract became the benchmark, which was quickly surpassed by Lemieux, only to see the Great One re-upped by McNall to $3 million. In the sixteen months after Gretzky's signing, the *Net Worth* authors counted eleven big-money deals, which also served to increase the going rate for hockey's foot soldiers. "There's no question the Gretzky contract catapulted the NHL salary scale," Bob Goodenow, then still just a player agent, told the *Toronto Star* in 1989. "There is an ability to pay that has been unlocked."[10]

The fact that Goodenow provided the classic example of unlocking the new-found riches available to NHL players by using the leverage of salary disclosure is not insignificant. He was the agent for Brett Hull in 1990, when the St. Louis Blues winger led the league in scoring

10. Quoted in Cruise and Griffiths, *Net Worth,* p. 334.

with seventy-two goals. Goodenow's strategy in winning Hull a three-year $7.3-million contract* — a huge raise from $125,000 — was described as "an education in negotiation" by another agent.[11] According to Dowbiggin, "Goodenow's skillful linking of Hull to Gretzky marked the genuine beginning of the salary spiral."[12] Other observers agree that Hull's rich contract showed how much money was available to players who were not free agents, and this provided the key to unlocking the NHL's ability to pay. Within two years Goodenow had left his agent business behind to take over the reins at the NHLPA. That's why the NHL is in such trouble financially and at the bargaining table.

Funny thing about Bruce McNall and Wayne Gretzky, however. Although the Great One was handed an unprecedented salary, he was underpaid even at $3 million according to calculations made by Cruise and Griffiths. The interest in hockey sparked by the superstar's arrival in southern California meant attendance at Kings' games soared to sellouts from the 10,000 level it had hovered at for years, and higher ticket prices boosted the team's gate receipts from $4 million to $13 million in short order. Increased advertising and broadcast revenues likely contributed to improving the Kings' cash flow by $7 million and $10 million annually, according to the *Net Worth* authors. McNall himself estimates that while he paid $18 million for Gretzky — only $2 million less than the $20 million he paid the previous owner, Jerry Buss, for the entire team in 1988 — the true value

---

* All figures used throughout the book are in US dollars except where noted.

11. Ibid., p. 371.

12. Dowbiggin, *Money Players,* p. 120.

of the Great One was more like $50 million.[13] From losing $4 million the season before Gretzky arrived, the Kings turned a profit of $13 million in 1989-90. Perhaps Bruce McNall was a visionary who saw the true financial potential of the NHL. Unfortunately for him — and the players — McNall ended up in prison himself, sentenced to six years for fraud in 1997. But not before selling the Kings for $113 million.[14]

HISTORY REPEATS ITSELF

The National Hockey League, according to one history, was founded out of spite in 1917 and built ever after on duplicity. By vanquishing all rivals, it finally appropriated in 1948 the cherished Stanley Cup, symbol of hockey supremacy, for which it once actually had to compete with other leagues. In *Deceptions and Doublecross: How the NHL Conquered Hockey,* authors Morey Holzman and Joseph Nieforth show how the league was founded by team owners of the old National Hockey Association (NHA) for the express purpose of ditching one of their fellow franchise holders. Eddie Livingstone, owner of the Toronto Blueshirts, was "hardheaded and stubborn," according to the authors, and in 1917 he was expelled from the league. In order to prevent the litigious Livingstone from pressing a legal claim to an NHA franchise, owners in Ottawa, Quebec, and Montreal — which then had two teams — the Wanderers and *les Canadiens* — decided to fold their seven-year-old league and start a new one. Thus was born the National Hockey League, which at first was an all-Canadian circuit, adding teams

13. Cruise and Griffiths, *Net Worth,* p. 333.
14. Dowbiggin, *Money Players,* p. 120.

in Toronto in 1918 (the Arenas, which became the St. Pats the next year and the Maple Leafs in 1927), Hamilton in 1920 (the Tigers), and Montreal in 1924 (the Maroons). Of the other original NHL franchises, the Montreal Wanderers had to fold after only six games in 1917 because their rink burned down, and the Quebec Bulldogs franchise joined play in 1919 and folded partway through the following season.

Teams had competed for the Stanley Cup since 1893, when it was donated by Lord Frederick Arthur Stanley, a former British parliamentarian who had taken a liking to the sport of ice hockey while serving as the Queen's representative in Canada, the ceremonial Governor General. Stanley's two sons took to the game, and every winter he had his staff build an outdoor rink on the grounds of his official residence in Ottawa, Rideau Hall. He sponsored a team known as the Rideau Rebels, which played against a team of real senators and members of Parliament and even traveled to Toronto in 1890 to play a three-game challenge series. Stanley became so enamored of the game that he paid $48.67 out of his own pocket to purchase a silver trophy he named the Dominion Hockey Challenge Cup in the fall of 1893 and first awarded to an unsuspecting team from the Montreal Amateur Athletic Association, which had won the country's amateur championship the previous season. By the following spring, when the first games were played for the Stanley Cup, as it became known, its originator had already returned to England at the end of his political appointment.[15]

For the next two decades the Stanley Cup was emblematic of amateur hockey supremacy in Canada and was

15. D'Arcy Jenish, *The Stanley Cup: A Hundred Years of Hockey at Its Best* (Toronto: McClelland & Stewart, 2001), pp. 11-13.

often awarded several times a year, with the Cup holders obliged to answer challenges that were approved by the trophy's trustees. In its earliest years, these trustees were Ottawa sheriff John Sweetland and *Ottawa Journal* editor Phil Ross, who had played hockey with Lord Stanley's sons, Arthur and Algernon. According to Stanley Cup historian D'Arcy Jenish, "pursuit of the Cup quickly took hold of the country and became a national passion."[16] The game became increasingly professionalized, first by the NHA, which had been founded in 1909 by Renfrew, Ontario, tycoon Michael J. O'Brien for the express purpose of winning the Stanley Cup for his team, the Creamery Kings. The affluent O'Brien, who made his millions from logging and silver mining, set out to assemble "the best team money could buy," and in the process began a bidding war for players that changed the game of hockey and transformed the Stanley Cup from an amateur trophy to an object of desire for rich and powerful sportsmen.

In his efforts to wrest the Stanley Cup from the grasp of the nearby Ottawa Senators, O'Brien embarked on the first free-agent spending spree in hockey, first agreeing to pay brothers Lester and Frank Patrick a combined salary of $5,000 to join his Renfrew team from Edmonton. Then O'Brien stunned the hockey world by paying the mercurial Fred "Cyclone" Taylor of the Senators the unprecedented sum of $5,250 for a twelve-game season stretched over two months. As Jenish notes, that was only slightly less than the $6,500 salary that baseball star Ty Cobb had recently signed for — to play 154 games over seven months.[17] O'Brien was the first team owner to

16. Ibid., p. 15.
17. Ibid., p. 64.

prove that the Stanley Cup is a prize that can't be bought but must be earned, because despite their high-priced stars, the Creamery Kings could finish no higher than third in the fledgling NHA. In 1912 he moved the team to Toronto, renaming it the Blueshirts before selling it to Eddie Livingstone in 1915. By then the Patrick brothers had returned west, where they founded a professional hockey league of their own — the Pacific Coast Hockey Association, with teams in Vancouver, Victoria, Seattle, and Portland. By paying big bucks to star players such as Cyclone Taylor, who became the cornerstone of the Vancouver Millionaires franchise, the PCHA repeatedly challenged for and won the Stanley Cup from NHA and NHL teams.

While Lord Stanley had originally donated his silver trophy for the amateur hockey championship of Canada, the increased professionalization of the game meant teams in the U.S. began competing for the Stanley Cup, which required a ruling from its trustees in 1915. "The Stanley Cup is not emblematic of Canadian honors, but of the hockey championship of the world," declared trustee William Foran, who by then had joined Phillip Ross as guardian of hockey's Holy Grail. "Hence, if Portland and Seattle were to win . . . they would be allowed to retain the trophy."[18] The PCHA soon folded, selling its players to the NHL for $258,000, and according to Jenish, "the Stanley Cup became the exclusive property of the NHL, not by decree or edict, but by default."[19] The international precedent had been set, and in 1924 the NHL expand-

18. Morey Holzman and Joseph Nieforth, *Deceptions and Doublecross: How the NHL Conquered Hockey* (Toronto: Dundurn, 2002), pp. 94-95.

19. Jenish, *The Stanley Cup,* p. 96.

ed to the U.S., placing a team in Boston (the Bruins) and collecting a $15,000 expansion fee in the process. The following year the league expanded south again, awarding Odie Cleghorn a franchise that began play in Pittsburgh as the Pirates. Cleghorn, a former NHL star player, paid a $12,000 expansion fee but also forked over $25,000 for players from the defunct western league.

The NHL dealt harshly with the first strike by hockey players. In 1925, when Hamilton Tigers players refused to suit up for the playoffs after finishing first in league play, which had been extended from twenty-four to thirty games without extra pay, the league simply moved the franchise to New York, where it began play as the Americans. In 1926 the NHL added two more teams in the U.S., awarding expansion franchises to Chicago (the Blackhawks) and Detroit (the Cougars), each of which paid $12,000 for membership in the booming circuit. The Cougars also paid $25,000 for the contracts of players from the former Victoria Cougars franchise in the PCHA, appropriating their nickname in the process. According to hockey historian Michael McKinley, Blackhawks owner Frederick McLaughlin paid the most of all — $200,000 — for the contracts of players from the defunct western league.[20]

In the late 1920s a new rival league demanded a chance to play for the Cup. The American Hockey Association had been founded in 1925 as a minor-league affiliate of the NHL, but its owners quickly developed major-league aspirations — and designs on the Stanley Cup. They bestowed major-league status upon their renamed American Hockey League, but NHL president Frank Calder

20. Michael McKinley, *Putting a Roof on Winter: Hockey's Rise From Sport to Spectacle* (Vancouver: Greystone, 2000), p. 118.

declared the upstart circuit an "outlaw" league and threatened a lifetime suspension for any NHL player who signed with the AHL. Chicago shipping and grain tycoon James Norris, a former amateur hockey player with the Montreal AAA, owned the AHL champion Chicago Shamrocks (which regularly outdrew the NHL Blackhawks in the city's new 16,000-seat arena, the Chicago Stadium), but he really wanted a team in the NHL and applied for an expansion team in St. Louis. The NHL turned him down and instead moved the faltering Ottawa Senators franchise to St. Louis, where it played one season as the Eagles before folding. Enraged, Norris petitioned the Stanley Cup trustees for a challenge series against the reigning NHL Cup-holders, the Montreal Canadiens.

The trustees accepted the challenge and ordered the NHL to schedule a Cup series with the AHL champions. Calder ignored the challenge, and the Cup trustees threatened not only to strip Montreal of the trophy, but also to launch legal — even criminal — action against the NHL, presumably for theft.[21] Backed against the wall, Calder pulled a backroom power play that ensured the Stanley Cup would forever after remain the plaything of the National Hockey League. According to Holzman and Nieforth, Calder and the NHL "stole" the Stanley Cup. "What went on behind closed doors was not reported, but the Chicago Shamrocks never got to play for the Stanley Cup."[22] Stanley Cup trustee Foran, who was the Ottawa Senators' representative on the NHL board of governors, was fired from that post. In a complex series of moves, Norris gained control of the NHL's faltering

21. Holzman and Nieforth, *Deceptions and Doublecross,* p. 316.
22. Ibid., p. 320.

Detroit franchise, which he renamed the Red Wings, and disbanded the Chicago Shamrocks. Stripped of its most powerful owner, the AHL returned to its former status as a minor-league affiliate of the NHL. Frank Calder died in 1943, but his quest for permanent NHL control of the Stanley Cup was realized posthumously five years later, as the authors of *Deceptions and Doublecross* outline.

> By 1948, original trustee Phil Ross was ninety-one years old, and after fifty-six years as a vigilant guardian of the trophy, he knew it was time to move on . . . He and fellow trustee Cooper Smeaton signed an agreement that allowed the NHL to take stewardship of the oldest trophy continuously competed for by professional athletes — for as long as the NHL remained the dominant league in the world.[23]

Those days may soon be numbered. If the NHL is not playing come springtime, it could hardly be considered the world's dominant league. But there will always be hockey, even if it is being played on ice rinks in Sweden, Slovakia, Switzerland, the Czech Republic, Finland, and Russia instead of in NHL arenas. As long as there is satellite television, hockey fans in North America will be able to watch the games too. Would it be too much to ask the NHL to allow the two best teams that are playing games when springtime rolls around to compete for the Stanley Cup? After all, it's not theirs — they stole it. If they don't

23. Ibid., p. 333.

CHAPTER 2

The Reserve Clause — Freeing the Slaves

In their long struggle with team owners for salaries that corresponded more closely to their real value as performers, professional athletes had to first overturn a system set up by the various sports leagues that bore some uncomfortable similarities to legalized slavery. Under the old "reserve" system, team owners in a league could get together and decide among themselves where in that league an athlete would play. The athlete could play nowhere else in the league, unless he was bought and sold by team owners like a piece of property, or traded from one team to another. It was a great system for owners, because if a player could only play for one team, he didn't have much bargaining power. That team was basically able to dictate contract terms and decide how much it would pay him.

The only problem with this system was that it was illegal. Antitrust laws passed in the late nineteenth century banned businesses that were supposedly competing against one another from conspiring together in a "trust" to keep prices artificially high and/or wages artificially low. The hated "reserve" clause in professional sports ruined the career of many a pro athlete who balked at being treated like property and refused to go along with the system.

Many a legal challenge was launched against the reserve system in professional sports over the decades, and along the way some small victories against it were won, but it wasn't until the 1990s that the reserve clause was finally done away with legally. A few pioneers now hold a hallowed place in the history of each major-league sport for their challenge to the reserve system, and every professional athlete earning big bucks today should pay homage to them regularly. In baseball it was Curt Flood who started the free-agency ball rolling. The St. Louis Cardinals outfielder balked at being traded to the lowly Philadelphia Phillies at the peak of his career in the late 1960s and launched a lawsuit against Major League Baseball that went all the way to the U.S. Supreme Court. In basketball it was Spencer Haywood, a college dropout who petitioned the courts to allow him to play in the NBA in 1970, opening the way for undergraduates and now even high schoolers to play in the league. In football, which didn't get real free agency until the 1990s, there isn't one player to thank, because a long list of players sued the NFL for their freedom, and in the end it was only by launching legal action as a group that they finally overcame the draconian restrictions of the reserve clause.

In hockey the choices for free-agency icon are even slimmer. Would it be Bobby Orr, who signed as a free agent with the Chicago Blackhawks in 1976 without compensation being sent to the Boston Bruins, which still held his NHL playing rights? Probably not — a lawsuit filed by Boston owner Paul Mooney was settled when Chicago agreed to send the ever-popular "future considerations" to Beantown in exchange for hockey's greatest player ever. Orr's career in Chicago fizzled due to his infamous knee problems, however, and no record of any compensation going to the Bruins has been found.[1] Would it be Dale McCourt, the Red Wings center who balked in 1978 at being awarded as compensation to the Los Angeles Kings after Detroit signed the Kings' free-agent goaltender, Rogie Vachon? The NHL quickly backed off and allowed McCourt to stay in Detroit after he threatened legal action, no doubt realizing it would lose any court challenge to its version of the reserve clause. Would it be Scott Stevens, the Washington Capitals defenceman who signed the first real big-money NHL contract as a restricted free agent in 1990, a four-year, $4-million contract with the St. Louis Blues? The Blues had to bite the bullet and send five first-round draft choices to Washington under the draconian compensation rules that the league then enforced.

But events the next year showed that the NHL's limited free agents weren't really so free to move around the league after all. When St. Louis went back into the free-agent market, signing New Jersey winger Brendan Shanahan to a two-year, $1.6-million contract, the league ordered St. Louis to send Stevens (whose contract made him a more valuable player than Shanahan) to New Jersey as compensation. This put the brakes on further big-money signings, and the players soon realized that the system of free-agent compensation Eagleson had negotiated with the league was at best a merry-go-round and at worst a no-win situation for them. It was only after they ousted the Eagle from his well-feathered nest and stood up for themselves by going on strike in 1992 that NHL players of a certain age finally won the right to unrestricted free agency.

---

1. Russ Conway, *Game Misconduct: Alan Eagleson and the Corruption of Hockey* (Toronto: Macfarlane Walter & Ross, 1995), p. 4.

The question of what the magic age of free agency should be in the NHL has been the subject not only of hard bargaining, but also of delicious irony. By keeping the age fairly advanced in terms of the career of a professional athlete — thirty-one or thirty-two years old — NHL team owners figured they had beaten back the big-money aspirations of players by keeping the number of free agents down. Instead, as Marvin Miller pointed out, the laws of supply and demand served to drive up the price of free-agent athletes because of that very scarcity. In the end, higher salaries for free agents have served to raise the roof on salaries for all veteran players under the system of salary arbitration.

At the other end of the age scale, the supposed salary cap on rookies that was trumpeted by the NHL in 1995 as a glorious victory in its war on payroll inflation has proven to be a joke of a different kind — this time on the owners. By raising the roof at both ends of the hockey salary structure — one end standing $10 to $11 million high for veterans and the other $3 to $4 million high for rookies — the salary scale for all players in between was effectively increased.

Free agency has proven the key to higher salaries in the NHL and other pro sports leagues, but the struggle fought by players to win their freedom has been a long and difficult one. As usual, therein lies a tale . . .

THE RESERVE SYSTEM

Once upon a time, there was no free agency in professional sports. Players were only allowed to play for one team in a league under what was called the "reserve" system. A player could either sign a contract to play for that team or else look forward to a career working as a gas jockey, stocking supermarket shelves, or ploughing fields on the family farm. Occasionally a new league would start up in competition with the established circuit and sign away its players at higher salaries, such as the American League of baseball in 1901, the American Football League in 1960, the American Basketball Association in 1967, and the World Hockey Association in 1972. But sooner or later the upstart league would either go out of business or negotiate a merger with the big league it was annoying. In either case, the bargaining power players had briefly enjoyed, which temporarily sent salaries soaring closer to market values, quickly evaporated and owners were again able to keep salaries artificially low under the draconian reserve system.

In each professional sports league, promising players of a certain age are "drafted" by one team, which gains the exclusive right to sign its drafted prospects to play in that league. As with free agency at the other end of a player's career, the age at which players can be drafted and play professionally has been the subject of dispute — and even legal challenge — in each league. The NHL's draft age was lowered from twenty to eighteen in the late 1970s after a legal challenge launched in 1976 by nineteen-year-old Ken "The Rat" Linseman.[2] While he was denied the right to play in the NHL as a teenager, Linseman spent his time profitably in the WHA while his lawsuit was decided, playing a season in Birmingham, Alabama, as a "Baby Bull" and leading the team in scoring despite missing nine games. The Birmingham Bulls, which began their WHA life as the Toronto Toros, were a team largely

---

2. Paul D. Staudohar, *Playing for Dollars: Labor Relations and the Sports Business,* 3rd ed. (Ithaca: Cornell University Press, 1996), p. 158.

stocked with underaged talent from the Ontario Junior A league. (Trivia question: How many Baby Bulls can you name? Answer at the end of this chapter.)

The annual "amateur draft," as it's called in hockey — or "college draft," as it's referred to in other pro sports that draw almost exclusively on U.S. colleges and universities for their talent — is where teams get together and divide up the best young players. By long-standing tradition, the worst team in each league gets first choice of the available players, and the championship-winning team always gets last pick, unless of course it has traded away its selection or lost it as compensation for signing another team's free agent. In some leagues, where teams have been known to actually lose games in order to get a higher draft choice, the worst teams go into a "lottery" to decide which team gets the first draft pick. The NBA has a draft lottery, which has in recent years become a spectacle in itself, and the NHL briefly used a similar system after the Mario Lemieux debacle of 1984, when Pittsburgh out-lost New Jersey in an embarrassing race to finish last in the league and win the rights to the scoring sensation from Quebec.

The whole drafting exercise is repeated several times, depending on how many "rounds" a league's draft has, which has also often been the subject of negotiation and even litigation. From then on, the drafted players are basically the property of the teams that have drafted them, and for many years players had few options if they didn't want to sign a contract for the salary being offered by the team that held their rights. Foreign leagues — such as those in Europe for hockey and basketball players, and in Canada for footballers — provided some playing alternatives, but they invariably paid much less than the big leagues in the U.S. During those brief periods in sporting history when there have been competing North American leagues, which would bid up salaries in an attempt to sign players, athletes had some bargaining power. But otherwise, drafted players had little choice due to the restrictive "reserve" clause that basically bound them to one team for life. Players could refuse to sign for the offered salary — or "hold out" in the parlance — but the only incentive for a team to offer a higher salary was its desire to add a talented player to its roster.

Hockey players in particular were vulnerable to exploitation under the reserve system because they tended to have the fewest employment alternatives outside of the sport. Most of the best players once came from Canada, where junior hockey was the traditional way to "make it" to the bright lights of the NHL. To play junior hockey, which operated under a similar reserve system of drafting promising younger prospects, most aspiring NHLers had to drop out of high school in their hometown and move to such junior hockey hotbeds as North Bay, Ontario, or Moose Jaw, Saskatchewan. Players who went the college route and enrolled in one of the big U.S. schools — which serve as virtual sports factories, turning out well-trained prospects for all the pro sports leagues — at least gained some level of education to fall back on, although many college athletes fail to complete their degrees and turn pro at the earliest opportunity.

Professional athletes long wondered why they should be subject to the restrictions of the reserve system. After all, in other fields of work a talented accountant or engineer could command the highest salary possible under the free enterprise system by negotiating a contract with the firm that valued that professional's services the most highly. Even other entertainers, such as actors, could negotiate with different filmmakers and sometimes sign for millions of dollars to star in just one movie. It seemed to many pro athletes that the reserve system only served to keep their salaries down, which sounded like an illegal restraint on trade. Under antitrust laws passed in both the U.S. and Canada, businesses were not supposed to be able to get together and form a monopoly — or "trust" — in order to dominate the market for a product or service. Antitrust laws, which have been applied much more successfully in the U.S. than in Canada, served since the early days of the twentieth century to break up some of the most restrictive trusts, such as large monopolies in oil, telephones, and railroads. Even into the twenty-first century, some were arguing that dominant firms in an industry — like Microsoft, which had virtually cornered the market for computer software — should be broken up.

It took a long time, but successive legal challenges and some hard bargaining in each of the major North American sports leagues have finally freed professional athletes from lifelong servitude under the reserve clause. As a result, players in each pro sport may now enjoy the financial fruits of free agency under certain conditions.

BASEBALL: BIRTHPLACE OF THE RESERVE CLAUSE

America's pastime is where the reserve clause originated, so it was only fitting that baseball was the battleground on which its restrictions were first fought and first defeated. Unfortunately for the players, there was a gap of about eighty-five years between the start of the fight and victory. Back in the earliest days of professional baseball, in the National League of the 1870s, players were free to negotiate with any team at the end of a season when their one-year contracts expired. This system of total free agency led to a bit of a merry-go-round, however, with rosters changing drastically from one year to the next. Competition between teams to sign the best players also tended to bid salaries upward, costing team owners money and keeping their profits down. In 1879, NL owners figured out a way to keep the best players from jumping from team to team and pushing salaries up in the process. The NL instituted a "reservation" system whereby each team was able to "reserve" five of its players at the end of each season. Those five reserved players could not sign a contract with any other team in the league, thus providing some roster stability and also keeping salaries down.

A funny thing happened when the National League first introduced the reservation system. The players didn't object, not the way they would decades later when they realized its economic implications. Quite the opposite — the first reservation of players produced a kind of star system. The five players reserved by each team at the end of a season came to enjoy an exalted status, with others on the team clamoring to be similarly coveted and reserved. Ironically, it was the players, not the owners, who pushed for the reserve clause to be included in every player's contract, binding him to that team for the next season.[3] And the next, and the next . . .

Soon, of course, it became obvious how the reservation system worked to the advantage of owners and to the detriment of players. If you could only sign a contract with one team, your bargaining power in seeking a raise was severely limited. By the late 1880s some teams were

3. G. Richard McKelvey, *For It's One, Two, Three, Four Strikes You're Out at the Owners' Ball Game* (Jefferson, NC: McFarland, 2001), p. 6.

making more than $100,000 in annual profit, which was huge money in those days. NL owners imposed a maximum salary of $2,000 a year, which was easily enforced due to the restrictive reserve clause that was now included in every player's contract. That salary cap, and complaints about playing conditions, led in 1885 to formation of the first players' association in pro sports — the Brotherhood of Professional Base Ball Players. The BPBBP didn't get very far in protesting against the reserve clause, the sale of players from one team to another, or the heavy fines often imposed by owners, so after the 1889 season it formed its own league in competition with the NL. The Players League only lasted for the 1890 season, but it introduced some forward-thinking ideas to the finances of the game. Gate receipts were shared equally between the home team and visitors in order to promote financial equality between clubs in large markets and those in smaller cities. Each team's revenue, after expenses, was shared equally between the players and stockholders, who had put up the money to finance the team.[4] In the end the Players League failed and the renegades filtered back to their NL teams, which imposed a ceiling of $2,400 on salaries. The BPBBP similarly expired, and for the next decade there was no players' association in baseball.

Players' only hope to escape the reserve clause was for a new league to start up and challenge the dominance of the established circuit. Then the players could exercise a bit of bargaining power by playing off one potential employer against the other. That's what happened in 1900, when the American League started up in competition with the NL. Not only did it offer higher salaries to

4. Ibid., p. 9.

players, but it also agreed to limit to five years the length of time a player could be reserved by a team. That promise proved empty, however, as the AL and NL merged three years later to create Major League Baseball as we know it today, with a World Series played annually between the championship-winning teams in each league. Included in the terms of merger was adoption by the American League clubs of the NL's hated reserve clause, which remained in force for more than seventy years thereafter.

History repeated itself in 1913 when the Federal League was formed and began signing players away from their AL and NL teams without regard for the reserve clause in each player's contract. This time, though, the story had a different ending. There had already been several successful legal challenges to the reserve clause, even before the AL-NL merger, so owners were well aware that their reserve system wouldn't stand up in court. The Federal League filed a lawsuit against organized baseball and the reserve clause in 1915, claiming it contravened the Sherman Antitrust Act of 1890. Major League Baseball settled the dispute by allowing Federal League teams in Chicago and St. Louis into the established circuit. That compromise didn't please everyone, however, and the owners of the Baltimore team in the Federal League, which had been excluded from the expansion of MLB, continued to press the antitrust action in an attempt to similarly land a big-league franchise. After several years, a district court finally agreed that organized baseball's restrictions violated antitrust laws and awarded backers of the Baltimore club $240,000 in damages. The verdict was overturned on appeal, and the case eventually went to the highest court in the land — the Supreme Court of the United States. That's where

MLB received its long-standing exemption from U.S. antitrust laws in 1922, after the court ruled that organized baseball was a "game" and not a business at all.

For decades, the legal precedent set by the decision in the Federal League case served as virtual immunity for Major League Baseball from legal challenges to its reserve clause. It also encouraged owners in other team sports to incorporate similar provisions into the contracts they offered to their players. Soon the player reservation system spread to all of professional sports. But while baseball was the venue for introducing the reserve clause, it was also the sport where the first victories against it came. When Curt Flood launched his lawsuit against Major League Baseball in 1969 and again took the reserve clause all the way to the U.S. Supreme Court, he didn't win the case, as many incorrectly assume — instead, he actually lost the court case, which had been bankrolled by the players' association in the hopes of winning free agency for its members. This convinced the players once and for all that the only way they could get rid of the reserve clause was by going on strike against it.

Flood's lawsuit, which had been thrown out of court and then thrown out again on appeal, was being considered by the U.S. Supreme Court even as player representatives voted unanimously to strike on March 31, 1972. The twelve-day strike that ensued, canceling eighty-six games, was fought over pension benefits. But when the players got what they wanted and the Supreme Court again upheld the reserve clause in the Flood case two months later, everybody knew the next player strike would be for free agency. The following year the restrictions of the reserve clause were relaxed by MLB, which agreed that any ten-year veteran who had spent the last five years with one team had the right to veto a trade. The 1973 collective bargaining agreement also brought players the right to salary arbitration after two years in the league — a compromise made by the owners in response to the players' demand for free agency.

When an arbitrator declared Oakland A's pitcher Jim "Catfish" Hunter a free agent in 1974, following a dispute with team owner Charles O. Finley over a deferred salary payment, the players realized that their new right to arbitration was what would blow open the growing cracks in baseball's reserve clause. The next season, pitchers Andy Messersmith of the Los Angeles Dodgers and Dave McNally of the Montreal Expos played without signing new contracts, after which an arbitrator ruled they were free agents and eligible to sign with any MLB team. In the 1976 collective agreement, in a bid to stem the growing tide of free agency, owners agreed to free players from the reserve clause after six years of servitude.

BASKETBALL: FREE AGENCY BY DEGREES

The sharpest bone of free-agency contention in roundball has been the college draft, which once prevented hoopsters from playing in the NBA until they had graduated college, or — more correctly, since many college players never get their degree — at least until their classmates had. But thanks to players like Spencer Haywood, who challenged that provision in court, players not only don't have to finish college; nowadays they don't even have to enroll. As a result of successive court challenges to the NBA draft, players may now jump right from high school into the big leagues. By comparison, the route to free agency for NBA players was relatively easy, coming through legal means in 1976 more because of the successes won by baseball players against the MLB reserve clause than by any stand taken by NBA players.

The free-agency battle in basketball revolved around the NBA's college draft and also an upstart league that had briefly challenged the big league's supremacy. The American Basketball Association (ABA) began play in 1967 as a colorful alternative to the NBA, featuring a multicolored ball and offering three points for field goals shot from long range. The ABA signed away some of the NBA's biggest names, including hot-shooting Rick Barry of the San Francisco Warriors. When the NBA went to court in an attempt to prevent Barry from signing with the cross-Bay Oakland Oaks, a court ruled the league's reserve clause was only valid for one year. Then Spencer Haywood, who signed with the ABA's Denver Nuggets as a college sophomore in 1969, jumped to the NBA Seattle Supersonics the following year. When the NBA ruled Haywood ineligible because he had never been drafted, he filed a lawsuit and won, which resulted in the league's "hardship" rule that allowed collegians to declare themselves eligible for the draft before they — or their class — had graduated.

By then the NBA was suffering an embarrassing losing streak in the courts of law in its attempt to corner the market for players on the courts of hardwood. When NBA star Oscar Robertson, who was president of the National Basketball Players' Association, launched an antitrust lawsuit against the league in 1970 in anticipation of a merger between the NBA and ABA, it set the wheels in motion for basketball free agency. The bidding war between the ABA and NBA caused the average salary in basketball to rise in just a few years from $20,000 to $140,000 as the new league signed such college stars as

Julius Erving to big-money contracts. The leagues did in fact merge in 1970, ending the bidding war, but Robertson's lawsuit took the free-agency fight from there. It was more than five years before the courts ruled that the NBA's system of compensation for teams that lost free agents, which worked to keep free-agent signings and thus salaries down, indeed violated U.S. antitrust law. In an out-of-court (legal or hardwood) settlement in 1976, the NBA agreed to phase in free agency over the next decade. In successive collective bargaining agreements, the present salary cap system was implemented as a counterbalance to free agency, and players were free to change teams upon the expiration of their contracts. The NBA draft, which now includes players coming right out of high school, has also been abbreviated by agreement to only two rounds.

FOOTBALL: THE RULE OF PETE ROZELLE

The National Football League Players' Association has been the tamest of the pro sports unions, at least since Bob Goodenow took over leadership of the NHLPA. Perhaps because of the large number of players on a team, the small number of games played, and the large number of available replacement players, union solidarity between NFL players has been lower than in other sports. As a result, team owners were for many years able to keep the free-agency and salary demands of players in check. Even until 1993 the NFL was able to get away without offering true free agency despite the legal victories won by players in other sports. The fact that the NFL was able to avoid free agency for so long is made all the more incredible by a 1957 Supreme Court ruling that, unlike Major League Baseball, football was not exempt from antitrust laws. However, due to the cunning of long-time commissioner Pete Rozelle, who ruled the league from 1960 to 1989, the NFL forestalled free agency for more than thirty years in almost total defiance of the law. It was only in 1993, after it failed to win free agency on the picket line, that the NFLPA went to court to once and for all win freedom for football players.

The secret to the NFL's success in beating back free agency for so many years was the so-called Rozelle Rule, which the commissioner invoked to deal with any signings by teams of another club's property . . . er, player. In the first years after the 1957 court ruling that the NFL was indeed subject to antitrust laws, the signing of free agents was discouraged by a "gentleman's agreement" between owners. That began to break down in the early 1960s, though, and a few free agents were signed by other teams. The system that Rozelle introduced to deal with these situations almost guaranteed they wouldn't be repeated. Under the Rozelle Rule, the signing club had to send compensation to the other team in the form of another player or players or, more commonly, one or more draft choices. If the teams couldn't agree on compensation, Rozelle would determine it himself. The compensation Rozelle awarded was usually so heavy that free-agent signings were rarely seen in the NFL for decades.

Several players attempted to challenge the system, including quarterback Joe Kapp, who had jumped from the Minnesota Vikings to the New England Patriots in 1970. In what one textbook describes as a "bizarre split decision," Kapp won his antitrust lawsuit against the NFL, but was awarded no damages by the court.[5] In 1972,

5. Michael Leeds and Peter von Allmen, *The Economics of Sports* (Boston: Addison-Wesley, 2002), p. 312.

NFLPA president John Mackey, a tight end for the Baltimore Colts, filed a class-action suit against the NFL for unfair labor practices and antitrust violations on behalf of himself and thirty-one other players. They won their case in district court, which ruled that the NFL had indeed violated antitrust law, and they won again on appeal. But the Mackey case took four years to wend its way through the legal system, and the NFL was prepared to pursue the matter all the way to the U.S. Supreme Court. Instead of gambling and grasping for the brass ring of free agency, the NFLPA, which was nearly bankrupt, settled the case out of court.

The players' association had fallen on hard times because a collective agreement had not been in place since 1974, which meant that it was not receiving union dues from teams for their players. The NFLPA was thus in survival mode and agreed to drop the Mackey case in exchange for a new agreement that recognized it as a union. Instead of free agency, the 1976 agreement only modified the Rozelle Rule to include a fixed compensation scale of draft choices instead of the arbitrary awarding of players. As a result of agreeing to these restrictions on free agency, over the next decade only two NFL players changed teams in that manner.

NFL players watched for years while the salaries of baseball and basketball stars soared under free agency, and they finally decided to go out on strike for the same privilege in 1987. Their brief walkout was soundly thwarted by NFL owners, who hired replacement players and resumed play as usual. NFLPA members slunk back to work, but resolved to win free agency in the courts if they couldn't gain it on the picket line. On the day the strike ended, NFLPA president Marvin Powell, an offensive tackle for the New York Jets, filed an antitrust case against the NFL. However, because the players had agreed in collective bargaining to the restrictions on their freedom in the form of free-agent compensation, the court ruled that they in effect consented to the antitrust violations the league would otherwise be guilty of. The only way they could win free agency legally was to dissolve the NFLPA, which they voted to do in 1988. After that, several players filed antitrust lawsuits against the league, which took several years to go to trial.

Sensing its vulnerability in the face of this tactic, the NFL reverted to Plan B — literally — and introduced some free-agency half measures that it hoped could be slipped past the antitrust laws. Plan B free agency, introduced by the NFL in 1988, allowed teams to protect thirty-seven players on their rosters and made the rest free agents without compensation. However, the compensation system remained in effect for teams that lost a protected player, and unprotected players tended to be third stringers, so salaries hardly went up at all in the few years that Plan B free agency was in effect. In 1992 that system ended when Jets running back Freeman McNeil, who had filed a lawsuit against the NFL on behalf of himself and seven other players, was successful in striking down Plan B free agency as a violation of antitrust laws. As a result, the NFL was obliged to negotiate a new system of free agency with a players' association that was quickly reconstituted for the occasion.

Some claim the NFL players again fumbled the ball by agreeing to a system that grants players free agency only after they have spent five years in the league — a period longer than the average career for pro football players. NFL free agency also still allows teams to protect one player as their "franchise" player, who cannot be signed by any other team. Perhaps as a result of these restrictions, NFL salaries are the lowest in the four major professional sports in North America, despite its being by far the most popular spectator sport with the most lucrative network television contracts. Of course, having fifty or more players on a roster, including practice squad players — instead of the dozen or so on basketball teams — keeps the average salary lower despite higher revenues and greater revenue sharing.

HOCKEY: AFRAID TO GO IN THE CORNERS

Free agency came haltingly in hockey, mainly because the NHL Players' Association for years was not militant enough to stand up to the owners and the reserve clause — or even stand up to its own hired executive director. Given the legal success professional athletes in other sports had in winning free agency, the NHLPA could likely have won freedom for its members many years before it did if it hadn't been for the duplicity of Alan Eagleson, who feasted off the ignorance of the players he supposedly represented. Eagleson blew two golden opportunities in the 1970s to win free agency for NHL players, first when the World Hockey Association started up in 1972, and then when it merged with the senior circuit seven years later.

Like the other sports leagues, the NHL had a reserve clause in its standard player contract for years, binding the player to a club for life — or until he was sold or traded. It was only when the WHA sprang up all over North America — with hopes of eventually expanding to Europe in a true "world" league — that the NHL's reserve clause was challenged in court. The WHA was founded by ABA originator Gary Davidson, and the impetus for its creation, according to economist Roger

Noll, was the rich profits being pulled down by NHL teams. Despite a lack of published financial data, Noll at the time counted only one money-losing franchise in the established circuit — Charles Finley's California Golden (née Oakland) Seals.

> Most of the NHL teams, including several expansion teams, are doing exceeding well. Some teams may even challenge the NBA's [New York] Knicks for first place in total profits. Furthermore, several hockey teams are in the super profitable category, which, perhaps, explains the formation of the WHA.[6]

The WHA immediately signed away several NHL stars, including Bobby Hull, Bernie Parent, Derek Sanderson, and Gerry Cheevers. Sanderson, a glamorous young center who languished on star-studded Boston's third line, saw his salary increase from $50,000 to $300,000 a year as a marquee attraction in the WHA. The new league signed sixty-six NHL regulars for its first season at an average salary of $53,000 — more than double what the average NHLer was then earning.[7] Their NHL teams went to court in an attempt to keep these players, claiming the reserve clause in the contracts they had signed obligated them to stay with the team for life. The courts found that the NHL's reserve clause applied only within the league and didn't prevent players from signing with a team in a different league if their contracts had expired. Following

6. Roger Noll, "The Team Sports Industry: An Introduction," in *The Government and the Sport Business,* ed. Roger Noll (Washington: Brookings, 1974), p. 198.

7. James G. Scoville, "Labor Relations in Sports," in Noll, *The Government and the Sport Business,* p. 198.

that decision, WHA teams raided NHL rosters at will, and for a time pro hockey players enjoyed salaries second only to those paid to NBA players. By 1976 the average NHL salary rose to $86,000 a year, compared with $78,000 in the NFL and only $51,500 in MLB.[8] Of course, given the laws of nature — not to mention economics — it couldn't last.

The WHA proved a tenuous enterprise financially, and its backers quickly realized that their best chance to challenge the NHL's supremacy was not on the ice but in court, following the antitrust example being pioneered in other sports. It launched an antitrust lawsuit against the NHL, which also came under investigation by the U.S. Justice Department for its monopolistic practices. According to the authors of *Net Worth,* the NHL had attracted the interest of regulators in the U.S. a year before the WHA came along, and the threat of legal sanctions against it became more real after the upstart circuit went to court.

> After a little more than one year of investigation, the Department of Justice concluded that virtually everything upon which the NHL was based — from the draft to the joint-affiliation agreement with minor-league teams — constituted a violation of one or more sections of the powerful Sherman Anti-Trust Act.[9]

Rather than fight a losing legal battle, the NHL agreed in 1974 to pay the WHA $1.7 million in damages for restraint of trade and also to play a series of exhibition

8. Leeds and von Allmen, *The Economics of Sports,* p. 226.
9. David Cruise and Alison Griffiths, *Net Worth: Exploding the Myths of Pro Hockey* (Toronto: Penguin, 1991), p. 270.

games between the leagues. In order to get on the right side of the law as far as the reserve clause was concerned, the NHL also that year replaced it with an "option" clause, which bound a player to his team for only one year after his contract expired. However, the option clause also stipulated that compensation be provided to teams that lost players as free agents, and the compensation scale set up was so onerous that few players changed teams without being traded. Of the 137 players who became free agents between 1976 and 1980, Cruise and Griffiths counted only twenty-three who changed teams, concluding: "In essence, the players had been as restricted as they had been under the reserve clause."[10]

By the end of the 1970s the WHA was on its last legs and pushing for a merger with the NHL, which was prepared to allow four of the WHA's healthiest franchises — Edmonton, Winnipeg, Hartford, and Quebec — into its ranks for the princely sum of $6 million apiece, which was declared an "expansion" fee.

The legal precedent for the antitrust implications of a merger between competing sports leagues had been established a few years earlier in basketball. After Oscar Robertson sued over the ABA-NBA merger, players won unrestricted free agency. The NHLPA's own law firm estimated that an antitrust suit against the merger had a "high degree of success" and could be used as a bargaining chip to win advances in free agency.[11] But as Cruise and Griffiths detail in Net Worth, Alan Eagleson did less than nothing in his position as executive director of the NHLPA to exploit the NHL's vulnerability on antitrust as a lever to win free agency. In fact, the Eagle persuaded

10. Ibid., p. 271.
11. Ibid., p. 285.

executive members of the players' association not to pursue free agency as a condition for merger by trotting out the long-standing plea used by owners to discourage players from demanding their rights — that such self-denial was "for the good of the game." Instead he encouraged them to settle for improvements to the league's pension plan — which the owners financed from a surplus built up in a plan that rightfully belonged to the players anyway. According to Cruise and Griffiths, this amounted to a "unilateral disarmament of the Players' Association."[12] Years later, NHLPA president Phil Esposito admitted to *Sports Illustrated* magazine that he had been "duped into serving as [Eagleson's] "puppet" during the merger talks.[13] Within a few years of the merger, the average NHL salary was half the average in the NFL, the lowest-paying of the three other major leagues, due to the NHL's restrictions on free agency.

It was only after NHL players dumped Eagleson that the NHLPA first used the strike weapon in its quest for free agency. Since then, hockey players' salaries quickly surpassed those of their colleagues in the NFL, even if the average $1.7 million NHLPA members earn annually trails that made by players in the NBA and MLB.

(Trivia question answer: The Baby Bulls were Ken Linseman, Mark Napier, Rick Vaive, Craig Hartsburg, Rob Ramage, Pat Riggin, Michel Goulet, and Gaston Gingras.)

12. Ibid.
13. John Papanek and Bill Brubaker, "The Man Who Rules Hockey," *Sports Illustrated,* July 2, 1984, p. 72.

CHAPTER 3

Walking the Line —
Strikes and Lockouts
in Professional Sports

When a bottom-scraping Keanu Reeves accepted coach Gene Hackman's offer, in the movie *The Replacements,* and started as quarterback for Hackman's pro football team, whose players had gone on strike, the scenario was taken from real life. NFL teams hired replacement players in 1987 and continued play for two weeks while members of the NFL Players' Association paraded with picket signs outside stadiums on Sundays, refusing to show up for work in their quest for free agency.

So even if a strike or lockout has been called, it doesn't necessarily mean that work has to stop or that "The Show" can't go on in pro sports. Depending on the applicable labor laws, management may be allowed to hire replacement workers — or players — and continue with business as usual. Well, almost as usual. When U.S. president Ronald Reagan deemed air travel an essential service and brought in replacement workers after air traffic controllers went on strike in 1981, things were a bit chaotic in the crowded skies over America for a few weeks as inexperienced air traffic controllers struggled to keep order. But Reagan succeeded in "breaking" the union, and to this day air traffic control is a non-union job in the U.S. That was a turning point in American labor history, as ever since then management has been less reluctant to call in replacement workers if it can, and union power has been greatly reduced as a result.

Could that happen in an NHL labor dispute? The NFL's use of replacement players allowed it to defeat the 1987 strike called by its players, but would such a tactic work in the event of an NHL shutdown? Do fans really want to pay $50 a ticket to watch two teams of players who couldn't make the pros otherwise? Most professional players of any skill are already under contract to an NHL team, whether they play in the big league or in the minors, so they are members of the NHLPA. Crossing a picket line of their fellow hockey players might be too much for management to ask, especially in a sport where players have a long memory and are bound by an honor code — and where on-ice retribution is just a high-sticking penalty or a career-ending hip check away.

Workers — or players — also have the option of turning the tables on their employers, going into business for themselves in the event of a strike or lockout. Labor history is full of examples of union members starting up their own businesses during a labor dispute — such as successful strike newspapers founded by journalists and printers — that turn out to be viable competitors to their former employers. Sometimes they stay in operation for years after the strike or lockout has ended, even putting the original enterprise out of business. Employee-run ventures have a long history of being conceived, growing, and thriving during labor disputes. Some of the best newspapers around, such as the *Toronto Star,* started life as "strike sheets" put out by striking journalists. Alternative employment opportunities, labor economics, and leisure choices may play a large part in determining just how long the shutdown of NHL play might last.

STRIKE OR LOCKOUT?

Everyone knows what a strike is, as we've all been inconvenienced in one way or another at some time by union members who withdraw their services in support of demands for higher wages or improved working conditions. Not everybody knows the origin of the word "strike." It's got nothing to do with baseball, but goes back to the days of yore when sailing ships were the primary form of world travel and the job of air traffic controller hadn't even been dreamed up yet. When things got so bad on board ship that the sailors were moved to protest conditions — if the captain had ordered a particularly harsh flogging or maybe reduced their rum ration — they would refuse to sail and take down, or "strike," the ship's sails.

Not every work stoppage is the result of a strike by unions, though. Both labor and management have the right in law to call a halt to production when a contract — or collective bargaining agreement — has expired and a new one can't be negotiated. When management is the side that pulls the plug, a work stoppage is called a "lockout" because often that's literally what happens. Workers show up to find that the doors are locked and they can't report for work even if they want to. Some would punch the clock if they could, even if their union colleagues voted to strike, because they might not agree with the decision and also because they have to pay their mortgages every month. To avoid having to pay those workers who do show up after a strike has been called, management will lock the doors, sometimes leading to a simultaneous strike/lockout that leaves open the question of which side started the shutdown.

Sometimes work can continue without a strike or lock-out, even if a new contract is not in place. That has happened several times in professional sports. Often the sides can't agree on a contract, but neither wants to go as far as to close down the business because they can't predict what will happen next. Instead they may prefer to use the threat of a strike or lockout as a bargaining chip in an attempt to force concessions from the other side. After a contract has finally been agreed upon — with or without a strike or lockout — its provisions are usually made "retroactive," applying to the time that workers did their job without a new contract.

A strike can sometimes take place when there is a signed contract in force if workers are upset about something, like the withdrawal of a benefit or the suspension of a colleague. This is called a "wildcat" strike and is typically strictly illegal, so management can go to court for an order that work must resume, and can even press criminal charges if the court order is disobeyed. A business hit by an illegal strike can also sue the union for damages incurred, such as lost revenue, as a result of the work stoppage. That's why wildcat strikes are generally short — a temporary protest more than anything else.

In pro sports labor disruptions, the 1994-95 NHL lockout holds the dubious distinction of being the second-longest shutdown of play due to a labor dispute in professional sports. The 191-day lockout by NBA owners in 1998-99 ranks as the longest to date. A 232-day strike in Major League Baseball lasted for a longer length of time than the NBA lockout, but that owner-player temper tantrum extended throughout an entire off-season, and fewer playing dates were lost than in basketball or hockey.

BRAND NEW RULES IN THE GRAND OLD GAME

Being the first big-league sport in North America, Major League Baseball has the longest history of labor unrest, dating back to the nineteenth century. The first players' association in professional sports, the Brotherhood of Professional Base Ball Players, went on strike for free agency in 1890, forming a rival league made up of 200 players who bolted from their National League teams. The upstart circuit lasted only a season, however, and players slowly drifted back to their NL clubs. Then in 1912 the irascible Ty Cobb was suspended for ten days after wading into the stands in New York to wale on a leather-lunged heckler. That incident prompted a brief strike by his Detroit Tigers teammates, who laid down their bats and gloves for one game in protest. In the wake of the strike, the Baseball Players' Fraternity was formed to not only protect the interests of players, but also push for higher salaries. It didn't get very far, dissolving in 1917 due to declining membership. For almost three decades afterwards there was no players' association in Major League Baseball, until the American Baseball Guild was formed in 1946. It managed to negotiate a minimum salary of $5,000 and also get a modest pension for retired players, but the guild was basically a "company union," dominated in negotiations by owners, and it did little to advance the real interests of players, such as pushing for free agency.

The Major League Baseball Players' Association that we know today was formed in 1952, and it too was a pushover for owners in negotiations until 1966, when the players hired Marvin Miller from the United Steelworkers of America as the union's executive director.

Miller took a more hardline stance against team owners and negotiated several breakthroughs for players in 1968 and 1970 contracts, including arbitration of grievances, such as disputes over the interpretation of contract language. He also persuaded players to refuse to sign their contracts prior to training camp in 1969 as a protest over the slow pace of pension talks. Then in 1972 the MLBPA went on strike for thirteen days in a dispute over pensions and health benefits. Owners expected the strike to end quickly and were unprepared for the new-found militancy of players. Hiring a professional negotiator like Miller had changed the rules of engagement in contract talks, and the solidarity that a veteran union leader brought to the players paid off in spades. The strike resulted in cancellation of the first nine playing dates of the 1972 season, costing teams $5 million in lost revenues over an issue that in the end was inexpensively settled. The strike ended with disbelieving owners capitulating in order to get the season finally started. The players' victory strengthened their resolve to stand up for their demands in future negotiations. The "iron rule" of owners was over, and a new era of player militancy — and riches — dawned. The following year Miller won yet another key contract clause for baseball players, this one providing for salary arbitration if a player's pay could not be agreed on in negotiations.

In 1976, amidst several legal challenges by individual players trying to win free agency through the courts, the MLBPA put the issue on the bargaining table in talks for a new collective agreement. The owners locked players out of training camp for seventeen days that spring before finally allowing regular-season play to commence while contract talks continued. Following several high-profile legal victories on the free-agency front, the two sides finally agreed to a new four-year agreement in July. For the first time it allowed players to become free agents under certain conditions. As more and more major leaguers went the lucrative free-agent route, teams realized they had to put the brakes on player movement somehow before salaries started going through the roof. When the agreement expired in 1980, owners demanded a compensation system for teams that had lost players through free agency in order to stem the tide of big-money signings. A strike appeared inevitable before the 1980 season, but the league opener was saved when both sides agreed to separate free agency from other issues on the bargaining table. They soon reached agreement on the other matters, but not on free agency, and a committee of players and owners was formed to study the question. A year later it hadn't resolved the problem, so owners announced they would unilaterally impose their own compensation scale. In response, the players decided to strike on May 29, 1981. Legal challenges delayed the player walkout for two weeks, but on June 12 that's just what major leaguers did, calling a halt to the 1981 season that was then in progress.

Unlike the situation during the 1972 strike, team owners were well prepared to deal with the MLBPA's hardline tactics this time around. They had been building up a $15-million war chest since 1979 and had also purchased $50 million in strike insurance from Lloyd's of London. By contrast, the players had little to fall back on and had to rely on union solidarity to hold together as the strike continued into a second month. Both sides dug in as negotiators Miller and Ray Grebey exchanged attacks through the media, which only served to harden resistance to settlement on both sides. Mediation did little to improve relations at the negotiating table, and as the strike continued past six weeks, the only incentive to settle seemed to be the ever-increasing likelihood that the entire season would have to be canceled if play did not resume soon. Finally, after fifty lost playing dates and 713 canceled games, both sides made the significant concessions needed for the signing of a new four-year contract. Free agency remained an option for players, but with increased compensation for the teams losing them. History shows that the players won the 1981 baseball strike because their salaries continued to increase. From an average of $185,000 in 1981, MLB salaries more than doubled to $371,000 four years later.

When collective bargaining couldn't reach a new agreement in 1985, players managed to win increased pension benefits with a two-day strike at mid-season. Owners were only able to gain a concession that players had to wait until their third year in the league to file for salary arbitration. Unable to keep salaries down at the bargaining table, owners attempted to do so by agreeing among themselves not to throw big money around to sign big-name free agents. After the MLBPA filed a lawsuit, the courts found the owners guilty of colluding to keep salaries down from 1985-87, and the average salary rose again, from $412,000 in 1987 to $597,000 in 1990. A thirty-two-day lockout by owners during spring training that year failed to win significant concessions from the players, and the average MLB salary rose to $851,000 by 1991. The following year it topped the $1-million mark, and by 1994 it had risen to $1.2 million.

The spiraling salaries in baseball led to the longest-lasting of all sports strikes in 1994. It lasted 232 days and caused the World Series to be canceled for the first time ever. Players walked out just as the 1994 pennant races were gathering steam. Fifty-two playing dates were canceled that season, as well as all post-season play. The strike extended twenty-five days into the 1995 season before the players agreed to a "luxury tax" on salaries, but not a salary cap as owners had been demanding. This half measure is even softer than a loophole-riddled "soft" salary cap. It merely discourages overspending on salaries by penalizing teams a percentage of their excess expenditures. Player salaries in Major League Baseball continued to climb despite the luxury tax won at such cost by owners, reaching an average of $1.4 million by 1998.[1]

In 2002, Major League Baseball narrowly averted what would have been its ninth work stoppage in thirty years when an agreement was reached hours before a strike deadline set by the players' association for August 30. By then, regular-season play was almost complete, and players had received most of their salaries for the season, but the playoffs and World Series loomed, increasing the pressure on owners to settle the dispute. Under the previous collective agreement, the luxury tax had not been levied for the preceding two years, and owners were anxious to reinstate this brake on spending, but players insisted on setting the bar as high as possible. Under the new four-year agreement, a luxury tax returned to baseball on team payrolls over $117 million in 2003, rising to $136.5 million by 2006.[2]

1. Michael Leeds and Peter von Allmen, *The Economics of Sports* (Boston: Addison-Wesley, 2002), p. 226.

2. Paul D. Staudohar, "Baseball Negotiations: A New Agreement," *Monthly Labor Review*, December 2002, p. 21.

BASKETBALL: A PAY SCALE FOR PRO ATHLETES

The players' association in the NBA was formed in 1954, and at first it was more of a mild-mannered professional body than a militant labor union. But in 1964 the National Basketball Players' Association (NBPA) threatened to boycott the league's annual all-star game in support of demands for a pension plan, to which the NBA agreed only after the game was delayed by several minutes. Three years later, at the start of the playoffs, the NBPA threatened to go on strike for medical insurance and an increase in pension benefits. The timing of the threat quickly brought about the demanded improvements, along with the first collective bargaining agreement in professional sports.[3] The NBPA was also certified under U.S. labor law as a trade union.

NBA players won free agency through a series of legal challenges in the 1970s instead of by striking, and even the league's salary cap was agreed to amicably in 1983, so basketball enjoyed relative labor peace for many years compared with other pro sports. Things changed in the 1990s, when NBA team owners imposed two lockouts in disputes over revenue sharing and the league's salary cap. In 1995 the dispute was resolved before the regular season began, so no playing time was lost. Owners wanted to make the league's soft salary cap into a "hard" cap by closing the loopholes that had made it relatively easy for teams to spend more than the allowed amount on player salaries. Players understandably balked at that

3. Paul D. Staudohar, *Playing for Dollars: Labor Relations and the Sports Business,* 3rd ed. (Ithaca: Cornell University Press, 1996), p. 107.

idea, and several stars, including Michael Jordan and Patrick Ewing, called for decertification of the union in a bid to gain free agency under U.S. antitrust laws.

The league imposed a lockout on June 30, which was conveniently after the playoffs had concluded and several months before training camps were to open in advance of the next season. A union decertification vote, which some of the league's biggest stars had been demanding, was soundly defeated, and a shutdown of league play was averted when the NBA dropped its demand for a hard salary cap. The 1995 NBA contract increased the percentage of revenues flowing to players from 53 percent to 57 percent and also included some revenues from luxury-box sales and licensing agreements. The deal was for a six-year contract that allowed the league to renegotiate after three years if salaries kept rising because the salary cap was ineffective. When Kevin Garnett of the Minnesota Timberwolves signed a whopping seven-year, $126-million deal that pushed the combined payrolls of NBA teams above 57 percent of league revenues, team owners voted 27-2 in March 1998 to reopen their contract with the NBPA.[4]

The NBA was well prepared to hold out in support of its demand that players reduce the percentage of league revenues they took home and locked players out at the start of the 1998-99 season to prove it. Commissioner David Stern had cannily included a clause in the league's television contracts that called for teams to receive revenues even if games were not played, although the money would eventually have to be repaid. For their part, players were unable to legally enforce the "guaranteed" contracts they thought would require them to be

4. Leeds and von Allmen, *The Economics of Sports,* p. 306.

paid in the event of a lockout. After a 191-day shutdown, the NBPA agreed in January 1999 to a new seven-year collective agreement that included the first "pay scale" in professional sports (described in Chapter 4). The agreement also limited combined team payrolls to 55 percent of league revenues until its final year, 2004-05, when the players' share of revenues would return to 57 percent.

FOOTBALL: MEET THE REPLACEMENTS

The NFL has suffered numerous strikes since the 1960s, and each dispute has been more acrimonious than the last. At first NFL players went on strike only during training camp, as the players' association struggled in the 1960s and '70s to gain recognition and win its first few collective bargaining agreements. But twice during the 1980s, NFLPA members went on strike during the regular season in fruitless pursuit of the free agency that had so enriched their colleagues in baseball and basketball. The militancy culminated in the calamitous strike of 1987.

Three short strikes and strike/lockouts took place between 1968 and 1974 as the NFLPA fought with the league to negotiate its first few collective agreements, but only training camp was disrupted each time and no playing time was lost. In 1968, training camps were shut down for ten days in a dispute over pension plan contributions before the NFLPA was able to sign its first contract with the league. The players held out of training camp for twenty days in 1971 before getting a second contract, and for forty-two days in 1974 without an agreement being reached. The NFLPA didn't get its third agreement with the league until 1977, a five-year deal that expired in 1982, setting the scene for the league's first shutdown of play.

By 1982 the NFLPA started to flex its muscles and become more militant under Executive Director Ed Garvey, whose leadership style has been described as "confrontational."[5] Under Garvey the players demanded that owners devote 55 percent of their gross revenues to salaries and pensions. The owners took a hard line in opposition and were prepared to hold out against a strike, having arranged for a $150-million line of credit to keep their franchises afloat. The players got nowhere at the bargaining table with their demand for a percentage of the league's gross revenues, so they switched to calling for a pay scale based on seniority and funded by television revenues. When this proposal was also flatly rejected by team owners, the NFLPA went on strike after only two weeks of the 1982 season had been played. Mediation failed to bring the sides closer together, and when the strike dragged on into November, the possibility loomed that the NFL season would have to be canceled if an agreement couldn't be reached. Finally, after some prominent players spoke out publicly against the strike, the NFLPA dropped its demand for a pay scale and accepted the league's offer of a compensation package worth $1.6 billion over five years. The fifty-seven-day strike had wiped out half the NFL regular season, so the league extended play for one week before holding its playoffs and Super Bowl as usual.

When the collective agreement expired in 1987, the NFLPA had a new leader in Gene Upshaw, a former offensive lineman with the Oakland Raiders. Negotiations with the league didn't start until the regular season had already begun in September. Owners basically stone-

5. Ibid., p. 301.

walled talks and called the NFLPA's bluff, almost daring them to strike, which they did two weeks into the season, on September 22. The league then played the ace up its sleeve in the form of replacement players, who were paid a flat $1,000 each per game. After a one-week hiatus, during which training-camp cuts were airlifted back into town for a few hurried practices, the games resumed with new men wearing the jerseys of regular players. The spectacle of previously unknown players showing up in the national television spotlight for such signature events as Monday Night Football resulted in some curious twists:

✧ TV ratings slipped only slightly for NFL games played with replacement players, falling to 11 or 12 rating points from their usual average of 15, due largely to the curiosity factor.

✧ Owners actually made more money per game during the strike due to their savings on players salaries, averaging $921,000 in profit compared with their usual $800,000 despite lower gate receipts.

✧ Attendance, which slipped a drastic 72 percent, from 60,000 to an average of 17,000 per game during the strike's first week, increased by the second week of the strike to 25,000.[6]

The owners' profits were only temporary, however, as the television networks were soon demanding a $60-million rebate from the league as a result of lost viewers and advertisers. NFL teams exempted their season ticket holders from paying full price to watch "scab" players run around on the field, so they had to eventually refund

6. Staudohar, *Playing for Dollars,* p. 75.

that money as well. The owners may have suffered financially, but not as badly as the striking players, who had not built up any strike fund from which to pay themselves wages during their holdout. NFLPA members were losing an average of $15,000 in salary per game and faced the possibility of losing their high-paying jobs permanently if owners made good on their threat to continue playing the entire season — and playoffs — with replacements. By the third week of the strike, defectors from the union ranks began crossing picket lines to suit up alongside the replacements, and by mid-October the NFLPA agreed to end the strike, asking in exchange only for the reinstatement of regular players. The beleaguered union had the last laugh on the league by going to court in 1993 to finally win the free agency it had been unable to achieve on the picket line.

HOCKEY: FIGHTING'S IN THEIR BLOOD

NHL players may until recently have been the least militant of all professional athletes in the modern era, but labor unrest in hockey actually predates the league's formation. Back in 1910, owners of teams in the old National Hockey Association, the NHL's immediate predecessor, decided to impose a $5,000 salary cap in a bid to limit their labor costs. There was no players' association back then, but some of the game's biggest stars fought the edict. Art Ross of the Montreal Wanderers protested that he and his teammates had been paid more than twice that amount annually ever since the league had been formed several years earlier. Ross led a revolt against the salary cap, and for a time NHA players threatened to form their own league. The protest fizzled, however, because NHA owners had all the big rinks under contract, meaning that if the players wanted to start their own league, they would have to play outside on frozen ponds. Art Ross was nearly suspended for his labor activism, and for the next half century any player who tried to negotiate demands with hockey team owners placed his career in jeopardy.

After the NHL was formed in 1917, players on its Hamilton Tigers went on strike in 1925 over playoff pay, and the league's response was swift and harsh. The team was sold to a bootlegger in the U.S., who moved it to New York City and renamed it the Americans. The NHL's union-busting tactics were finely honed over the years under the guidance of big-business owners such as Bruce Norris of Detroit and Bill Wirtz of Chicago. Ted Lindsay, a star with the Red Wings (owned by Norris), was traded to Wirtz's perennial also-ran Blackhawks in 1957 as punishment for heading the newly formed NHL Players' Association. For a decade the NHLPA got almost nowhere in negotiations with team owners, other than to establish a minimum salary and set up what the players thought was a Cadillac pension plan. Then in 1967 the players' association hired as its executive director Toronto lawyer and player agent Alan Eagleson, who managed to finally gain formal recognition for the union and to negotiate its first collective agreement. But for years the NHLPA was hampered because Eagleson was playing both sides of the table to further his own interests.

After Eagleson was acrimoniously ousted in 1992, he was replaced as NHLPA executive director by Detroit labor lawyer and agent Bob Goodenow, who was anxious to demonstrate a new union militancy and player solidarity following the NHLPA's pushover years under the Eagle. The previous agreement had expired before the 1991-92 season, but the league had dragged its feet in negotiations during the NHLPA's change in leadership.

Realizing that the playoffs were when owners made most of their money from higher ticket prices and increased television revenues, while the players made next to nothing compared with their regular-season salaries, Goodenow called a strike vote as league play drew to a close. NHLPA members voted 560-4 to walk out, and the strike started on April 1, delaying the start of post-season play. The dispute was settled ten days later when the NHL made minor concessions on salary arbitration, licensing rights, and playoff pay, but the players' most significant gain in the three-year deal was the drop in age for unrestricted free agency from thirty-one to thirty. This substantially increased the number of free-agent hockey players and set the stage for a showdown when that agreement expired.

The players were happy with the new free-agency rules, which caused the average NHL salary to more than double from $263,000 during the 1990-91 season to $558,000 three years later, so they agreed to play the 1993-94 season uninterrupted while negotiations continued, even if a new agreement could not be reached. After playing an entire year without a new deal, however, all bets were off. The NHL had hired New York lawyer and former NBA executive Gary Bettman to replace John Ziegler as commissioner following the ten-day strike in 1992, and his mandate was to bring a salary cap to hockey as he had done in basketball. Bettman was anxious to prove his mettle in negotiations at the first opportunity, just as Goodenow had been upon taking the reins at the players' association. In an effort to force concessions from the NHLPA, the league locked out players at the scheduled start of the 1994-95 season in October. The NHL's demand was not exactly for a salary cap, except on the salaries of rookies, which had been rising out of control. Instead it took the form of a "payroll tax," similar to the luxury tax in baseball, and would have had the effect of redistributing revenue from the rich, free-spending teams in big markets, such as New York and Detroit, to those in small markets, such as Calgary and Edmonton. The NHL produced data to show that its teams had lost a combined $67.8 million in the previous two years, while player salaries had jumped to an average 61 percent of revenues from 42 percent in 1990.

The NHLPA refused to budge, and as the strike dragged on into 1995 and players pursued other opportunities — signing to play for teams in Europe or barnstorming together across North America — the owners had to decide whether to cancel the NHL season for the first time or abandon their quest for control over labor costs. In mid-January the NHL dropped its demand for a pay-roll tax after a 103-day lockout during which 468 games were canceled, settling for a salary cap only on rookies in an attempt to bring down entry-level salaries. Free agency was also restricted under the agreement until players reached age thirty-two, although it would fall to age thirty-one in 1997. The age for salary arbitration was increased to twenty-six or twenty-seven, depending on a player's age when he entered the league. The collective agreement was set for six years and saved the season, which resumed with a reduced schedule of only forty-eight games instead of the original eighty-two.

The funny thing about the 1994-95 NHL lockout is how most "experts" concluded, even years later, that the league had won a significant victory over the players' association. The leading textbook on sports economics states that "the union blinked" in 1995 and that NHL owners successfully stood up to the players' association "in order to impose limits on player salaries."[7] The leading expert on labor relations in sports judged that "the owners clearly won" the dispute by getting agreement on a rookie salary cap and increased restrictions on free agency.[8]

Gary Bettman and NHL owners were just as confident as the experts that they had put the brakes on rising player salaries, but time, their own greed, and the ingenuity of agents have proven them cruelly incorrect. The average salary continued to skyrocket following the 1995 agreement, to $892,000 by 1996 and to $1.167 million two years later. By the time the collective agreement expired in 2000, the average NHL player was making $1.43 million a year, and two years after that it was $1.79 million. The players have turned out to be the clear winners of the 1994-95 lockout, and the NHL lost badly, bungling an opportunity to put the players in their place once and for all. That's why, a decade later, the league so desperately needs the players' capitulation on a salary cap — to save the owners from themselves. To get it, they might be prepared to risk everything.

7. Leeds and von Allmen, *The Economics of Sports,* p. 317.
8. Staudohar, *Playing for Dollars,* p. 152.

CHAPTER 4

Salary Caps — Hard, Soft, and Laughable

Gary Bettman is generally acknowledged to be the "father" of the modern salary cap in professional sports, so it's no surprise the NHL has given him a mandate to impose one in hockey. Bettman was a young commissioner-in-training at the NBA head office in the early 1980s, standing third in the league's executive hierarchy behind commissioner Lawrence O'Brien and deputy commissioner David Stern, when he came up with the idea of placing a cap on salaries to resolve a contract impasse that meant most of the 1982-83 NBA season was played without a collective bargaining agreement. Owners wanted a mechanism to restrain the growth of salaries that were even then considered to be spiraling out of control at several hundred thousand dollars a year, but players understandably balked at the idea. They threatened to go on strike before the playoffs began if an agreement could not be reached by April 1, 1983.

The dispute was settled after Bettman suggested the league offer to share with players a percentage of team revenues while capping total salary expenditures at a percentage of gross league income. The NBA at first offered to share 40 percent of its revenues with the players, but they weren't buying the idea of owners taking home half again more money than they did. The league then upped its offer to a 50-50 split of revenues, and ultimately, under the threat of a late-season strike that would have cut off the NBA's high-paying playoff television revenue, NBA owners finally agreed to let the players have more than they would get — 53 percent of revenues. The agreement was reached on March 31, 1983, the eve of the players' strike deadline, and the salary cap was born, with Gary Bettman listed on its birth certificate as father.

Since then, every major professional sports league in North America has instituted — or in the case of the NHL, is attempting to impose — some form of salary cap as a means of keeping player salaries down.

BASKETBALL: PAYBACK TIME

The NBA salary cap first went into effect during the 1984-85 season, with the payroll limit calculated at $3.6 million per team. That immediately created a problem because five teams were already paying out more than that amount in salaries. Their payrolls were frozen, but the popularity of basketball led to greatly increased revenues — mostly from ever-richer network television contracts — so the NBA salary cap doubled to $7.2 million for the 1988-89 season. By 1992 it had almost doubled again, to $14 million, bringing salaries up to an average of $1.2 million from $340,000 at the advent of the salary cap eight years earlier.[1]

The NBA salary cap, to the benefit of players, was a "soft" cap because for many years teams could pay out

1. Paul D. Staudohar, "Salary Caps in Professional Team Sports," *Compensation and Working Conditions*, Spring 1998, p. 4.

more than the stated limit on salaries due to several gaping loopholes in the collective agreement. For example, NBA teams were allowed to re-sign one of their own players at any salary, which would not count against the league's salary cap. This was called the "Larry Bird rule" because it was first used by the Boston Celtics to re-sign their biggest star. Celtics management complained in the mid-1980s that the new salary cap would result in its having to break up a team of star players, many of whose contracts were due for renegotiation. An amendment was added to the salary cap clause in the collective agreement, and it was soon exploited by other teams desperate to sign that one missing piece they felt was necessary to bring them a championship. For example, the Portland Trailblazers signed free-agent center Chris Dudley to a multi-year contract in 1993 that paid him only $790,000 in its first year, but contained a clause that allowed him to become a free agent after only one season, after which they re-signed him as a returning player for $4 million a year. Under the precedent set by the Celtics in re-signing Bird, that contract wouldn't count against Portland's salary cap. The Miami Heat then used the same tactic in signing center Alonzo Mourning away from the Charlotte Hornets. David Stern, who by then was NBA commissioner, went to court in 1995 in an attempt to prevent this obvious evasion of the league's salary cap, but the lawsuit failed to stop the chicanery.

In negotiations for a new collective bargaining agreement in 1995, the NBA attempted to close this and other loopholes and turn the league's soft salary cap into a hard one that teams would be penalized for exceeding. The NBA Players' Association (NBPA) countered by demanding removal of the salary cap altogether, along with abolition of the league's college draft. The players had received legal advice that these devices used by the league to limit salaries and restrict free agency were in violation of U.S. antitrust laws. But according to legal precedent, as long as the players had agreed to limitations on free agency through their union in collective bargaining, they were an allowable restraint on free trade.

Several of the league's biggest stars, including Michael Jordan of the Chicago Bulls and Patrick Ewing of the New York Knicks — who, of course, had the most to gain from loosening salary restrictions — led a movement to decertify the NBPA. That would have had the effect of nullifying the bargaining relationship between players and the league, bringing the law's antitrust provisions into force. NBPA members narrowly voted against decertifying their union after the league agreed to drop its demand for a hard cap, to increase the percentage of revenues flowing to the players from 53 percent to 57.5 percent, and also to include in the shared revenues a slice of luxury-box proceeds, which the owners had kept for themselves previously. As a result, NBA salaries soared to an average of $2.2 million by the 1997-98 season and the league's salary cap rose to $25 million per team.[2]

By 1998 the NBA salary cap had proven so soft that it did little to slow down salary escalation, which led owners to demand that the loopholes be plugged in a new collective agreement. To prove they were serious, they locked players out at the scheduled start of the 1998-99 season, and the dispute dragged on for 191 days before an agreement was reached. The result of the shutdown was a "pay scale" that limited salaries based on a player's number of years in the league and that more closely

2. Ibid.

resembled a hard salary cap. Players who had been in the league for five years or less would be limited to $9 million a year, players who had five to ten years of experience were limited to $11 million, and veterans of more than ten years were capped at $14 million annually. In addition, the "Larry Bird rule" was severely restricted by limiting to 12 percent the salary increase that a franchise player could receive. Big-money contracts that had already been signed, however, were "grandfathered" or allowed to continue in place under the agreement despite exceeding the pay scale. The agreement also limited combined team payrolls to 55 percent of league revenues until its final year, 2004-05, when the players' share of revenues would return to 57 percent.

In its attempt to finally get a handle on player salaries, the system instituted by the NBA in 1999 as a result of its lengthy lockout also included a 100 percent luxury tax on payrolls and other measures that made it almost incomprehensible to the average fan — not to mention the average player. Believe it or not, to ensure players are not overpaid, the NBA's current salary cap first requires they pay back 10 percent of their salary. That money goes into an escrow fund that acts as a kind of fudge factor — the players may or may not get that money back, depending on whether total league payrolls go over the limit. *Profit* magazine tried its best recently to explain the system.

If total salaries did not exceed 55% of Basketball-Related Income (BRI), then all of that money is returned to players. If salaries are more than 61.1 per cent of BRI, then none of it comes back. Should salaries fall anywhere in between, the amount under 61.1 of BRI is returned. If salaries go over 61.1 % of BRI, then the luxury tax kicks in for teams which individually go over the amount. For every extra dollar a team overspends, a dollar goes to the league in luxury tax. That money is then portioned out to every club in the league, though the amount still depends on how much a team has spent. Those teams over the 61.1 threshold receive less than everyone else, which effectively multiplies the penalty.[3]

Got that? The upshot, according to *Profit*, is that during the 2003-04 season, player salaries totaled about 65 percent of NBA revenues. Suffice it to say that the players didn't get their 10 percent back from the escrow fund. Even the convoluted provisions of the 1998 salary cap/ luxury tax failed to stop NBA salaries from going through the roof, and by 2004 estimates pegged the average at $4.9 million, or almost double the next-highest major-league average salary, which was $2.5 million for Major League Baseball. As a result, NBA owners are serving notice, just like the NHL has done, that they want a salary rollback of major proportions when the league's collective agreement expires in 2005.

FOOTBALL: IS THERE A CAPOLOGIST IN THE HOUSE?

It took until 1993 for genuine free agency to come to the National Football League, but when that was achieved, the owners quickly agreed to revenue sharing which the players had been demanding as part of any salary cap agreement. The league agreed to share a minimum of 58 percent and a maximum of 62 percent of revenues with players. Due to greatly increased television revenues taken in by the NFL since then, each team's salary cap has

3. Paul Jay, "How Open Books Saved the NBA," *Profit*, March 2004, p. S16.

more than doubled over the past decade, from $34.6 million in 1994 to $80.6 million for the 2004 season.

To offset that upward influence on salaries, the NFL Players' Association had to agree to a hard salary cap that penalizes teams exceeding it, often with the forfeiture of coveted college draft choices. As a result, the annual frenzy of free-agent signings in the NFL that begins on February 15 is matched only by the frenzy of salary dumping that takes place starting on June 1 every year as teams release players in a mad scramble to stay under the salary cap. Players who were signed to big-money contracts as free agents only a year or two earlier may suddenly find themselves being forced to renegotiate their salary downwards or risk being cut adrift to make room under the salary cap for the team's latest free-agent signings. Veterans who lose their starting positions are particularly vulnerable to becoming victims of the NFL's version of the salary cap as rather than keeping them as experienced backups, teams typically target them first to place on waivers in order to clear "cap room." They are usually replaced by lower-priced young players who may not be ready to step in and perform as well as the experienced veteran would be if needed due to injury. If he is able to catch on with another team, the veteran player may be forced to go from earning millions to toiling for the minimum salary payable to veteran players — a measly few hundred thousand dollars — because other teams rarely have room under their own salary caps to afford more high-priced talent once the season starts.

The NFL salary cap has also created an entirely new category of team executive, the "capologist." His job (yes, they are all men) is to perform the unnatural mental contortions required to figure out how to stay under the league's mandated maximum for player salaries. The capologist must be part accountant, part lawyer, part economist, and part magician to navigate the rules surrounding the league's hard cap. As unforgiving as the NFL salary cap is, however, capologists have still found innovative ways to soften its impact, or at least defer its consequences. The one loophole they have to work with, aside from cutting players they can no longer afford, is the salary cap's provision for spreading signing bonuses over the life of a player's contract, up to a maximum of six years. Thus players are often offered a huge signing bonus up front that far exceeds their annual salary, allowing the team to soften the same-year impact of the new player on the team's salary cap. Because NFL contracts are not guaranteed, unlike in other professional sports, this gives the team the option of releasing the player — and jettisoning his salary — a year or two later if he doesn't live up to expectations. The player gets to keep the signing bonus, which frequently comes back to haunt the team in more ways than one.

The problem is that when NFL teams repeat this exercise several times over, it leaves a lot of deferred bonus money still counting against their salary cap years later, often long after a player has moved on as a free agent to another team or two. The Dallas Cowboys, one of the NFL's top teams of the mid-1990s, were among the first casualties of this salary cap syndrome. As a result of the escalating salary demands of their star players following repeated Super Bowl success, the 'Pokes were forced to renegotiate the contracts of several and had to wiggle their way under the NFL's salary cap by including huge signing bonuses spread over many years. By the 2001 season, Dallas had $25 million counting against its salary cap that had already been paid to players who were no longer on its roster.

Besides complaining about the annual signing and dumping of players that resembles a game of musical chairs, many fans moan that the salary cap has essentially brought about the demise of the great NFL dynasties. Teams that win several successive Super Bowls, such as the Pittsburgh Steelers in the 1970s, the San Francisco 49ers in the 1980s, and the Cowboys in the 1990s, are no longer possible under the league's salary cap. Teams simply cannot keep a roster of great players together because the NFL's hard salary cap dictates how many of their stars the most successful teams are able to afford.

BASEBALL: A TAX ON LUXURY

In Major League Baseball, the system used to limit owners' spending on salaries for free-agent players is not a salary cap at all, but instead a luxury tax on payrolls that penalizes teams exceeding a budget limit. Owners began demanding a salary cap in 1989 in a bid to slow down rising salaries for free agents, offering in exchange to share 43 percent of gate receipts and broadcasting revenues with players, although these monies amounted to only 82 percent of total team revenues. The owners locked players out of spring training for thirty-two days prior to the 1990 season without getting their agreement on a salary cap, and the average MLB salary more than doubled over the next four years, from less than $500,000 to more than $1.1 million.[4]

By the time the 1990 collective bargaining agreement expired four years later, team owners were prepared to shut down America's pastime to back up their demands for a salary cap and a 50-50 split of revenues. That set the

4. Staudohar, "Salary Caps in Professional Team Sports," p. 9.

stage for the longest interruption yet of a pro sports league, as MLB Players' Association members voted to strike with less than two months remaining in the 1994 season rather than give in to the ultimatum by owners. Shortly after the strike began, owners modified their demand from a salary cap to a luxury tax that would levy a penalty on payrolls that exceeded a certain percentage of average team revenues. The tax would be collected by the league and redistributed to teams with less demonstrated ability — or willingness — to pay high salaries. The MLBPA balked at that proposal as well, viewing it as a "salary cap in disguise." The impasse forced cancellation of the 1994 league playoffs and, for the first time ever, the World Series. The scheduled start of the 1995 baseball season also passed without a resolution to the dispute. It was almost a month later before players finally agreed to a modified luxury-tax proposal after a 232-day shutdown of play.

The luxury tax levied a 35 percent penalty on team payrolls exceeding $51 million starting in 1997. This was raised to $55 million the following year. Proceeds from the luxury tax are put into a fund paid out to small-market teams that are less able to afford the high salaries paid to free agents. Baseball's luxury tax did little to deter the free-spending ways of owners intent on achieving the ego gratification of winning the World Series, however. The expansion Florida Marlins celebrated the luxury tax's introduction in 1996 by immediately embarking on a spending spree, paying out $89.1 million for six free agents who helped them win the World Series. That December, fourteen teams spent a total of $216 million to sign twenty-eight free agents in one week. In the first two years after the luxury tax was implemented, the New York Yankees' payroll topped $60 million each year, requiring owner George Steinbrenner to pay a hefty tax bill to MLB head office. As a result of such spending, the average MLB salary rose by almost 25 percent in 1997, from the $1.1-million range it had hovered in for the previous four years, to $1.38 million. The luxury tax was lowered to 34 percent in 1999 on an increased payroll limit of $58.9 million. Under the 1994 collective agreement, no luxury tax was to be levied in the final two years of the contract, which expired in 2001, in the hope that salaries would have stabilized by then.

That wasn't what happened, however, as baseball's average salary continued to climb, hitting $1.4 million by 1998, standing at almost $1.9 million by 2000, and topping $2.3 million by 2002.[5] By then owners were prepared to put their collective foot down and demand not only that the luxury tax be reinstated in the next agreement, but also that the tax rate be increased in an attempt to halt the salary spiral. Baseball commissioner Bud Selig claimed that teams had lost a collective $511 million in 2001 and that only five teams had turned a profit, although the players' association disputed that claim. Selig asked for a luxury tax of 50 percent on payrolls over $98 million, which would have immediately placed the New York Yankees, baseball's highest-paying team, $37 million over the limit and liable to pay $18.5 million in tax. The players proposed that the luxury tax apply on payrolls above $125 million in 2003, rising to $145 million by 2005. In the end, agreement was reached on a six-year collective agreement that set the payroll limit at $117 million in 2003, rising gradually to $136.5 million by

5. Adam Conn, "Baseball Average Salaries from 1998-2003," *ContractBud.com,* December 24, 2003, http://www.contractbud.com/?article=apc_baseavgsalary

2005. The luxury tax was set on a sliding scale that penalized repeat violators of the payroll limit more harshly than first-time transgressors. A team's first violation of the payroll limit in the agreement's first year, for example, was set at 17.5 percent, but by the fourth year repeat offenders could be taxed as much as 40 percent on their excess expenditures. As a result, baseball salaries actually began to come down by 2004, falling 2.7 percent from the average of $2.56 million per player the previous year.

HOCKEY: ROOKIE MISTAKES

As the only major sports league without a salary cap or luxury tax, the NHL brought Gary Bettman in from basketball for the express purpose of implementing just such a system of spending restraint on player salaries. Team owners even gave Bettman the title of commissioner, which conferred increased status and power over previous league heads, who had always held the title of president. The 1994-95 NHL lockout was an attempt by owners to impose a salary cap, or at least a luxury tax on team payrolls similar to baseball's system of redistributing money from high-spending franchises to small-market teams. NHL players balked at such a system and held out into January, which threatened cancellation of the season and the Stanley Cup playoffs. In the end the owners blinked and settled for a salary cap on rookies only, in an attempt to put the brakes on player costs. But if the NBA's original salary cap was a softie, then the NHL rookie cap is so full of holes that it resembles Swiss cheese.

The salary cap on rookies under the 1995 agreement was supposed to be $850,000, rising annually to $1.075 million by 2000, but cunning agents and compliant general managers conspired to find so many loopholes that it has become a standing joke and an insult to the idea of spending restraint. Before the NHL and NHLPA completed the agreement that introduced the rookie salary cap, Paul Kariya signed his first contract with Disney's Mighty Ducks of Anaheim for $6.5 million over three years, or an average of more than $2 million per season. That was a more realistic market value for top NHL draft choices than the scale set by the new collective agreement, and it was only a matter of time before player agents found a way to get that kind of money for their fresh-faced clients.

Boston Bruins general manager Harry Sinden, who had never before been known for throwing around money, was the first management culprit. He signed top draft choice Joe Thornton to a contract that provided for a salary at the rookie maximum of $925,000 a year in 1997, but the bonuses included in Thornton's contract took his annual compensation well above $2 million. Under the collective agreement, eleven categories of bonus money were allowed for rookie skaters. Mike Barnett, Thornton's agent, convinced Sinden to include rich bonuses for easily achievable feats, such as $250,000 for receiving a given amount of ice time. Barnett, who has since gone over to management as general manger of the Phoenix Coyotes, also included a clause providing for multiplier "balloon" bonuses that increased Thornton's compensation several times over if he achieved more than one bonus. For example, if he met benchmarks in two of his bonus categories, he received a $1.8-million balloon bonus, which quickly hiked his compensation package above what Kariya had received before the NHL's rookie salary cap was invoked. Thornton's landmark rookie contract also allowed the balloon bonuses to "roll over" from year to year. If he didn't get the bonus one year, he could still get it the next. Thornton struggled as an eighteen-year-old rookie playing against grown men, receiving only a $250,000 ice-time bonus his first year. By his third season, though, the big center was a force in the league, and he pocketed more than $3 million in rolled-over bonus money that year.[6]

After Barnett and Thornton exposed the loopholes in the NHL's rookie salary cap, it was like feeding time in the shark pen as agents used the precedent to extract lucrative — and imaginative — contracts for their clients. Vincent Lecavalier, the NHL's first overall draft choice in 1998, negotiated an incentive-laden pact with the Tampa Bay Lightning. Lecavalier's base salary was only the $975,000 allowable that year under the rookie salary cap, but if he eventually achieved all of the roll-over bonuses contained in the three-year contract, it was estimated he could earn almost twice as much as Thornton. The complex deal, which was negotiated for Lecavalier by his agent Bob Sauve, a former NHL goaltender, listed six bonus categories in his first year, including his placing in rookie-of-the year voting, and five categories per year thereafter. Achieving each category, such as scoring twenty goals in a year, would earn Lecavalier an extra $250,000 a year, for a possible total of $3 million in his first year and $2.5 million the next two seasons. If Lecavalier only won the bonus for two of the five or six categories — such as for points, plus/minus rating, or even ice time — he got paid for them all. In addition, if Lecavalier somehow failed to make two bonus categories in one year, the potential payoff rolled over to the next

6. Bruce Dowbiggin, *Money Players: How Hockey's Greatest Stars Beat the NHL at Its Own Game* (Toronto: McClelland & Stewart, 2003), p. 192.

season. As a result of such liberal bonus provisions, the lanky center was in a position to earn a total of $10 to $11 million. That wasn't all. If Lecavalier somehow won the league's scoring title or most valuable player honors in his first three seasons (admittedly an unlikely prospect for such a young player), or even was named the most gentlemanly player or best defensive forward, he stood to collect bonus money potentially worth another $4 million, for a potential total windfall topping $15 million. He didn't win those lofty honors, but he cashed in nicely just the same.

The Lecavalier contract, following as it did on Thornton's budget-busting deal, served as a standard for years afterward as top prospects enjoyed the new-found good fortune for rookies. Junior sensation Mike Comrie had Edmonton Oilers general manager Glen Sather over a barrel because Sather hadn't signed Comrie after his draft year in 1999, and Comrie would become a free agent if the Oilers didn't lock him up before the 2001 draft. Comrie got a rookie deal that earned him $3.5 million in bonuses. The next year it was the expansion Atlanta Thrashers' turn to pay, as they signed two high-priced rookies to contracts loaded with performance bonuses. Dany Heatley cashed in to the tune of $4 million while Ilya Kovalchuk earned $4.375 million.[7]

Instead of holding down salaries by placing restraints on rookie contracts, the 1995 collective agreement had accomplished exactly the opposite by fueling the imagination of agents. If they were undeterred by a rookie salary cap in what they could ask for their teenaged clients — who were restricted to negotiating with only one team, after all — agents were inspired to demand the

7. Ibid., p. 194.

moon for veteran free agents who held more promise of bringing short-term success to NHL teams. As a result, the average NHL salary escalated from $730,000 before the 1995 agreement to $1.17 million by the time Joe Thornton was a rookie two years later. When Vincent Lecavalier's three-year contract expired in 2001, the average NHL player contract was paying $1.43 million per annum.

SALARY-CAP EFFECTS

The dampening effect that salary caps were supposed to have on team payrolls has materialized to a greater or lesser degree in different leagues depending on how such restraints have been implemented. The NBA, which pioneered the concept thanks to Gary Bettman, has had the most experience with the process and has fine-tuned its salary cap over the past two decades from a crude, sieve-like provision filled with gaping loopholes. The elimination of some of these loopholes and the imposition of a pay scale and an escrow fund in the 1998 collective agreement were supposed to tighten up the NBA's salary cap, but the average league salary has still soared until it is now almost double the average in the next-highest-paying league. The artificial restrictions imposed by the NBA's salary cap have produced some idiotic results, such as teams trading players based more on the "cap value" than on their playing talent. Because player contracts in the NBA are guaranteed, unlike those in the NFL, teams cannot simply release players to get under the salary cap. Instead, general managers must find another team with "cap room" that is willing to take their unwanted players — and their inflated salaries.

Another off-season sideshow in the NBA has been the bidding for the star free agents of a rival team — perhaps a team in the same conference — which is designed to get the rivals into salary cap "trouble," as noted by sports economist Roger Noll.

The more subtle aspect of the salary cap is its effect on bidding strategy. If a team has a total salary amount below the cap, another team can force it to reach or go above the cap by offering a pay increase to a star player who is certain to have the offer matched by his current team. This maneuver diminishes the ability of the team retaining the player to operate in the free-agent market or to sign a rookie draft pick.[8]

Needless to say, the high-finance games of personnel management played off the hardwood courts of the NBA have become almost as important to team success in the standings as the traditional ingredients of player talent and coaching.

In the NFL, the hardest salary cap in all of sports has only brought mandated mediocrity, not to mention a roster merry-go-round on which players move from team to team before the season every year. The "parity" of competition that the salary cap has brought to football often seems more like a "parody" of competition, as teams yo-yo up and down in the standings from year to year depending on the results of their free-agent signings.

8. Roger G. Noll, "Professional Basketball: Economic and Business Perspectives," in *The Business of Professional Sports,* eds. Paul D. Staudohar and James A. Mangan (Urbana, IL: University of Chicago Press, 1991), p. 38.

The enforced end of dynasty teams brought by the "winner's curse" that comes along with free agency and payroll limits has done away with some of the allure of NFL football, yet it remains by far the most popular spectator sport worldwide, judging by its television revenues.

In baseball, the luxury tax has until recently proven a total joke and had little effect on either salaries or competitive balance, as the rich still get richer and continue to pay inflated salaries to stars in hopes of bringing a World Series championship to their hometown.

Economists have researched the effects of salary caps in professional sports, which has led to some interesting discoveries. Paul Staudohar, a sports labor relations expert, concluded that the imposition of artificial restraints on salaries is actually quite pointless because salaries are instead determined by market conditions such as attendance, television revenues, and stadium deals. "Salary caps and payroll taxes may seem beneficial to owners, but their effects appear to be more symbolic and cosmetic then fundamental."[9]

Economist Stefan Kesenne found that while they do serve to bring down player salaries, caps also tend to depress league revenues, which cancels out the benefits for owners. After studying the question, Kesenne was moved to wonder what was the point of salary caps in the first place.

On average, the players lose and the owners gain by a salary cap, but from this analysis it is clear that the players' losses out-balance the clubs' gains so that total league revenue, i.e. the revenue of all clubs together,

9. Staudohar, "Salary Caps in Professional Team Sports," p. 10.

diminishes . . . If a salary cap is causing a social loss . . . the question arises why it should be imposed.[10]

The most pronounced effects seem to be an increase in competitive balance in a sports league by spreading talent out more evenly and preventing rich teams in large markets from stockpiling talent.[11] The flip side of the "competitive balance" coin, as demonstrated by the NFL, is "mandated mediocrity." But even under a cap, as has been seen in most sports, and particularly in baseball with a luxury tax, rich teams will find ways around the restrictions and continue to outspend small-market clubs. "Because the cap is not consistent with profit incentives for teams, there are enforcement problems for big-city teams who have incentives to spend more than the cap," according to Roger Noll, who studied the NBA experience, "and for small-city teams, who have incentives to spend less than the cap."[12]

Whether a salary cap would save the National Hockey League from self-destruction is arguable, but there may be less draconian and more cooperative methods of achieving the same end.

10. Stefan Kesenne, "The Impact of Salary Caps in Professional Team Sports," *Scottish Journal of Political Economy,* September 2000, p. 427.

11. Michael Leeds and Peter von Allmen, *The Economics of Sports* (Boston: Addison-Wesley, 2002), p. 257.

12. Noll, "Professional Basketball," p. 38.

CHAPTER 5

Revenue Sharing — Major-League Socialism

The term "revenue sharing" has two meanings in the business of professional sports. Owners can enter into revenue-sharing agreements with their players or among themselves. Usually they do both, to a greater or lesser extent, but not in the NHL — and that might be at the root of the league's money problems.

Ironically, it doesn't seem to be how much revenue owners agree to share with players that determines how high salaries go. Studies have shown that the more revenues owners share among themselves, the less they end up paying their players, and thus the more they make in profit. "The result that revenue sharing reduces talent investment is long established," a pair of sports economists noted, "and follows simply from the dulling of incentives to win."[1]

However, the greedier the owners in a league are, refusing to share any or much of their revenue with other teams — such as in the NHL — the more they end up

1. Stefan Szymnski and Stefan Kesenne, "Competitive Balance and Gate Revenue Sharing in Team Sports," *Journal of Industrial Economics,* March 2004, p. 170.

spending for free agents in hopes of cashing in on a winning team and making even more money at playoff time. Sellout crowds paying higher ticket prices and increased television revenue for post-season play can often make the difference between a profitable season and red ink for NHL teams. But gambling big on high-priced free agents will backfire on most teams each year as they are eliminated from the Stanley Cup race (as demonstrated by the New York Rangers). Instead of cashing in, they end up losing money as a result of their greed. And NHL owners have shown over and over again just how greedy they are.

The National Football League is by far the most popular spectator sport in North America, and it capitalizes on that popularity big time, with television contracts that bring in billions of dollars annually. NFL owners share that money equally in a revenue-sharing system that has been described as something akin to socialism, and they also split gate receipts 60-40 between the home and visiting teams. As a result, there is more of a collective spirit and less cutthroat competition in the NFL — at least off the playing field. Perhaps not coincidentally, player salaries in football are the lowest of all the major North American sports, despite its being the marquee attraction, at least in the largest market, the U.S.

The demonstrated success of revenue sharing in keeping player costs down in the NFL has been studied by economists, who have found that this phenomenon has a basis in theory. The secret is in reducing the "incremental value" of free-agent players by eliminating the additional revenues that signing them can bring. "In general, the smaller the share of revenue going to the home club, the lower the incremental value of winning," noted economist

Gerald Scully, "and hence the lower the incremental value of superior player performance."[2] The net effect of socialism for teams, he concluded, is to reduce the salaries of players.

> If players are free to move between clubs and the division of revenues is 100-0, a player's pay tends to rise to the expected incremental revenue to the club of that player's performance. If players are free to move and the division of revenue is 50-50, there is no relationship between player salary and incremental value.[3]

The rationale advanced publicly for owners to share their revenues with each other is usually the motherhood concept of "competitive balance." Leagues that have greater revenue sharing tend to have teams that are more equal in the standings as well. The question of which teams will end up in the Super Bowl every year has become a crapshoot, depending on which NFL executives can best divine the voodoo economics inherent in the league's salary cap. But off the field, according to economists, the net effect of revenue sharing between teams is to allow owners to keep more revenues for themselves by discouraging them from paying it to free-agent players. One study of revenue sharing in basketball found that instead of the much-ballyhooed competitive balance that revenue sharing is claimed to produce, its effect tends to be more profit-oriented.

2. Gerald W. Scully, *The Market Structure of Sports* (Chicago: University of Chicago Press), 1995, p. 70.

3. Ibid., p. 69.

Revenue sharing among teams paradoxically does not affect competitive balance among teams, but it leads to the exploitation of players. The salary cap and the cost-sharing collusion of the NBA predictably lead to the least competitive balance of the three leagues over the period studied.[4]

In the NHL, revenue sharing between teams is the lowest of all the major leagues. Home teams keep all of the revenue from ticket sales without sharing it with their visitors. The league's 1999-2004 television contract with ABC provided $50 million in revenue annually, although that was dwarfed by the NFL's contracts with CBS, ABC, and Fox, which together bring the league $1.6 billion, with another $600 million in cable revenues. Basketball and baseball also far outstrip the NHL in television revenues, with the NBA pulling in roughly $766 million a year and MLB earning $559 million. Hockey teams are mostly left to fend for themselves with local or regional cable deals, the proceeds from which they also keep entirely for themselves. For large-market teams in hockey hotbeds, these television revenues can be substantial, but for those in small or new hockey markets they are often negligible. As a result, not only do teams in large, hockey-mad markets, such as in the northeastern U.S., make the most money; they also keep most of it for themselves without sharing it with teams in smaller markets that have less income. In this highly competitive business model, the rich, big-market teams end up spending most of those profits — and

4. John Vrooman, "The Economics of American Sports Leagues," *Scottish Journal of Political Economy,* September 2000, p. 394.

sometimes more — on salaries for free-agent players, often from the rosters of small-market teams that can't afford them any more. If NHL owners learned to share a little bit better among themselves, perhaps they wouldn't find themselves frittering away most of what they make by inflating the salaries of free agents.

When the NFL's competitive — or non-competitive — practices came under Congressional scrutiny just prior to the league's first in-season strike in 1982, union head Ed Garvey urged in his testimony at hearings into the issue that Congress "take a long hard look at revenue sharing because it has hurt the player market pool."[5] It's the ultimate irony in sports — socialism, not capitalism, leads to exploitation of the workers. Go figure.

THE SHELL GAME OF SHARING

Whether owners are sharing revenues among themselves or with their players, figuring out how much revenue there is to be shared is like trying to nail Jello to a tree. In these days of Enron-style creative accounting, getting to the bottom of the finances of big-league sports teams can be almost impossible. Several notable attempts have been made by sports economists and financial journalists, however, and the results are useful when pondering the supposed plight of beleaguered NHL teams, most of which are operated as private companies and are thus not required by law to disclose their finances publicly. As economist Gerald Scully notes, separating fact from fantasy in the accounts of privately owned sports fran-

5. Ed Garvey, quoted in David Harris, *The League: The Rise and Decline of the NFL* (New York: Bantam Books), 1986, p. 539.

chises can be difficult due to a decided lack of transparency, if not outright dishonesty.

> Fearing political scrutiny of their business practices, the teams tend to over-state expenses and understate operating profits in public pronouncements. Stated losses from operations are often a figment of creative accounting. It is not unusual for a club, even one with a losing record located in a small market, to generate a positive cash flow while its books show red ink.[6]

Not only do team owners try to hide money when it comes time to share revenue among themselves, but of course they also try to plead poverty when it comes to sharing it with their players. The trade-off each sports league usually has to agree to in order to wrest a salary cap or luxury tax from its players at the bargaining table is sharing a percentage of team revenues with them in salaries. Thus the dollar amount of each team's salary cap or payroll limit depends on what percentage of their revenues team owners are prepared to share with players. But simply agreeing on a percentage figure often doesn't settle the question, because exactly what is to be included in the pie that owners are willing to share with players is frequently a matter of dispute. Whether the revenues to be shared include such outside, or "ancillary," revenues as luxury-box proceeds or stadium-naming rights, for example, can make a difference amounting to millions of dollars on the salary cap.

Being sharp businessmen — which is generally how they got rich in the first place — team owners will

6. Scully, *The Market Structure of Sports,* p. 116.

attempt to keep for themselves as many of the dollars that they take in as they possibly can, by fair means or foul. Professional athletes are starting to demand an honest accounting of the proceeds attributable to their endeavors. If indeed a salary cap comes to the NHL — or a luxury tax that also redistributes prosperity from have to have-not teams — you can be sure that the players' association will demand its fair share of revenues from the league. The differences between how the spoils are divided in each sport are significant and can affect the fortunes of teams both on and off the playing surface. The hotly contested issues of revenue sharing in other sports perhaps foretell the future of the NHL once the dust settles on a new collective bargaining agreement.

BASEBALL: THE STEINBRENNER EFFECT

Like other professional sports, America's pastime has always been something of a shell game as far as finances are concerned, but ever since revenue sharing entered the baseball equation a decade or so ago, Major League Baseball's accounting practices have become positively surreal. Corporate tax laws long ago rendered most team profit-and-loss statements largely fictional, as owners have tended to take earnings out as salary to avoid paying tax on the money twice — once as corporate income and again as personal income. One textbook example is the Los Angeles Dodgers, which were owned for many years by the O'Malley family. As one of the most successful franchises in one of the largest sports markets in the U.S., the Dodgers by all rights should have been among the most profitable of MLB teams. Instead they regularly ranked in the middle of the pack because of their huge "administrative costs." Rather than taking their profits after the team had paid corporate income tax on them, the O'Malleys paid themselves huge salaries and wisely only paid tax on the money once. This resulted in a mediocre "book profit" for the Dodgers, which came nowhere close to being an accurate portrayal of the team's actual prosperity.

All kinds of accounting tricks have long been used by sports teams to keep the official bottom line low, such as building expensive stadiums and charging heavy depreciation against income, or borrowing huge sums and using that interest expense to decrease operating income.[7] With the advent of revenue sharing in the 1990s, Major League Baseball owners found even more creative ways to fudge their finances. To some owners, sharing what they have with less-prosperous businessmen is too much like socialism for their tastes. To others, the concept borders on communism. It seems most owners prefer the tried-and-true methods of capitalism, such as fiddling the account books to make it look like you're losing money when in fact you're raking it in by the yard. Yet even as owners cry poverty due to the outrageous salary demands of baseball players, the prices they are able to command for their franchises — should they decide to sell — keep going up by tens and hundreds of millions of dollars, and player salaries keep pace. Should we believe what they say or what they do?

Thank goodness for investigative journalists like Michael Ozanian, who has made a career of probing the finances of baseball and other sports, first for *Financial*

7. Michael Leeds and Peter von Allmen, *The Economics of Sports* (Boston: Addison-Wesley, 2002), pp. 90-91.

World magazine and more recently for *Forbes*. In considering the true financial health of a sports league, according to Ozanian, fans should not swallow what owners tell them but watch what they get for their franchises when they sell. In one special assessment for the *Wall Street Journal,* Ozanian and Kurt Badenhausen disputed the dire warnings of a "blue ribbon" panel in 2000 that baseball was headed toward financial ruin due to escalating payroll costs.

> The best way to analyze an industry's prospects — especially one that is, like baseball, dominated by privately held businesses — is by looking at asset values, not by pulling numbers from income statements. Paul Beeston, baseball's current president, once said that "under generally accepted accounting principles, I can turn a $4 million profit into a $2 million loss and I can get every national accounting firm to agree with me."[8]

Thanks to Ozanian, then-acting commissioner Bud Selig had to back down in 1994 on his claim that nineteen of the twenty-eight MLB teams were losing money. *Financial World* published an analysis that showed stadium revenues — from luxury boxes, advertising, and concession-stand sales — provided an ever-increasing proportion of team incomes. Broadcast revenues from television and radio still supplied the bulk of team incomes, according to Ozanian and Brooke Grabarek, but stadium revenues had risen from one-quarter as much as broad-

8. Michael K. Ozanian and Kurt Badenhausen, "Baseball Going Broke? Don't Believe It," *Wall Street Journal,* July 27, 2000, p. A22.

cast revenues in 1990 to almost two-thirds as much only four years later. As a result of adding those incomes to the bottom line, they calculated the number of big-league clubs with financial problems was only five, not nineteen as Selig claimed.[9] Selig publicly withdrew his original estimate of financial ruin, which he claimed was based only on projections, but he continued to insist that at least a dozen teams were in financial straits.[10]

Revenue sharing among owners in baseball came to the game only after Selig — himself part-owner of a small-market franchise in Milwaukee — began arguing in 1993 that leveling the financial playing field was the only way for the sport to survive. Fixing the fractured economics of the sport, Selig argued, required rich teams in large markets, such as the Yankees in New York, to share their revenues with teams such as his. The theory was that giving small-market teams a better chance at signing free agents would also give them a better chance to compete on the field, thus helping to restore competitive balance and thereby popularity to the game, whose fortunes had been declining for several years. The proposal was tied to the players accepting a salary cap in negotiations for a new collective agreement to replace the one that expired in 1994. In the end it took a 232-day shutdown of America's pastime to reach a deal with the players that included some form of salary restraint, and even then it was only a luxury tax, and not the salary cap that owners had been demanding.

9. Michael K. Ozanian and Brooke Grabarek, "Foul!" *Financial World,* September 1994, p. 18.

10. "Selig changes tune," *The Globe and Mail,* August 9, 1994, p. C7.

When baseball finally resumed play partway through the 1995 season, owners had agreed to share 43 percent of team revenues with players in the form of a $51-million payroll limit per team. The tax for exceeding this limit was set at 35 percent. At the same time, however, the owners could bring themselves to share just 34 percent of their own revenues with each other. Selig's proposal to bring financial and thus competitive parity to Major League Baseball was thus only partially successful. But being forced to share even a minority of their income with other teams has caused some owners to seek more creative ways around the requirement. According to Ozanian, this time writing in *Forbes,* owners skirt the revenue-sharing rules by setting up broadcasting arms that scoop up most of the earnings from television rights. By signing a sweetheart deal with their own cable companies to broadcast games, owners can keep most of the revenue not only out of the clutches of players, but also away from their fellow owners. Under this model, major-league teams become that much more valuable to broadcasting firms, several of which have bought baseball teams — and other sports franchises — in order to profit from these "synergies."

George Steinbrenner, who owns the high-rolling Yankees, pulled in $252 million in revenue in 2002 — almost double the MLB average — but he only had to share $29 million of that, or about 12 percent, with his fellow owners. According to *Forbes,* that's because the bulk of Yankees' broadcasting revenues accrue not to Steinbrenner, but to Yankee Entertainment and Sports Network. The YES Network, which is 60 percent owned by Steinbrenner, paid the team only $52 million in broadcast rights for the Yankee games, but it turned around and sold them to area cable firms and advertisers for $200 million, most of which goes directly to Steinbrenner, not to his fellow owners or to the player payroll. As a result of such creative thinking, *Forbes* estimated the value of Steinbrenner's Yankees at $850 million in 2003, up 13 percent from a year earlier.[11] The idea is catching on, according to Ozanian.

> The Red Sox do it, the Los Angeles Dodgers do it and so do the Atlanta Braves, the Chicago Cubs and the Toronto Blue Jays. The Twins will launch their network next year. The Houston Astros and the Chicago White Sox may do the same. The new cable channels could make the richest teams even richer, increasing the disparity between them and the weakest teams in the league.[12]

The Dodgers are owned by global media magnate Rupert Murdoch, who counts the Fox Network among his assets. The Braves are owned by Ted Turner, who owns the TNT network. The Cubs are owned by the Chicago Tribune Company, which also owns television stations. The Toronto Blue Jays, which are 80 percent owned by Canada's largest cable company, Rogers Communications, reported an operating loss of $20.6 million in 2001. But according to *Forbes,* the increased value to Rogers of being able to carry the Jays' games across Canada was enough to increase the team's worth the following year by about 20 percent, to $182 million.[13] The owner of the Red Sox also owns 80 percent of the New

11. Michael K. Ozanian, "Inside Pitch: How Baseball Team Owners Dupe the League's Revenue-Sharing System," *Forbes,* April 28, 2003, p. 64.

12. Ibid.

13. Kurt Badenhausen, Cecily Fluke, Lesley Kump, and Michael K. Ozanian, "Double Play: Why a Moneylosing Baseball Team Is Worth $700 Million," *Forbes*, April 15, 2002, p. 92.

England Sports Network (NESN) and thus avoided sharing revenues of $11.2 million, according to *Forbes*.[14]

As a result of this shifting of financial fortunes off the books of baseball teams, MLB's shared revenues amounted to only about 5 percent of total revenues, nowhere near the 34 percent originally agreed to, according to Ozanian. Baseball's "blue ribbon" panel — which was convened in 2000 to come up with ideas to save the game — called for revenue sharing to be increased to 60 percent in an attempt to prevent on-field domination by rich teams like the Yankees, who drive up free-agent salaries. But four years later, the real percentage of revenue sharing among owners was going down instead of up. "Despite Selig's best efforts, capitalism is going to triumph over socialism," concludes Ozanian. "It's good business for the owners — but not so good for Selig's revenue-sharing plan."[15]

BASKETBALL: THAT'S NOT REALLY REVENUE

In the mid-1990s, the NBA claimed that more than half of its teams were losing money and that the league as a whole was in the red. In the midst of the 1998 NBA lockout, however, Ozanian did an "exhaustive analysis" of club revenues and found that only ten of the NBA's twenty-nine teams lost money, not sixteen as the owners were claiming. The claimed losses were grossly exaggerated through "selective accounting," according to Ozanian, because teams were failing to include some extremely lucrative sources of revenue in their income. "It all comes down to how you define revenues," he wrote in *Forbes*. "Owners exclude most of the revenues

14. Ozanian, "Inside Pitch."
15. Ibid.

from stadium naming rights and advertising, luxury suites and team merchandise stores."[16]

Forbes surveyed 113 professional teams in the four major sports leagues and found that while many owners were pleading poverty, a hard look at the facts told quite a different story. While most pro sports franchises were unwilling to provide figures and open up their account ledgers — and especially their accounting practices — to public scrutiny, *Forbes* was able to make informed estimates by using available data, including television contracts, players' salaries, and stadium rent. In performing its analysis, it also relied on the best estimates of consultants, investment bankers, stadium operators, and trade publications to come up with what it called "solid estimates" of the financial positions of every franchise in the four major professional sports leagues, including the NHL.

The picture that emerged was of a $7.9-billion industry in which owners made $479 million in profit — or at least "operating income," which consists of earnings before interest, taxes, depreciation, and amortization of assets, such as rinks and arenas (EBITDA). That amounted to an average profit margin of 6 percent, which is unimpressive until you consider that it includes some teams that lose millions of dollars a year. Also, the operating income declared by teams failed to count some highly profitable and fast-growing "ancillary revenues," noted *Forbes*. These include one-time fees paid by corporations to have stadiums named after them, licensing fees paid by merchandisers for the right to use team logos on apparel, and advertising revenue from the billboards that adorn every stadium and arena nowadays and even intrude onto play-

16. Michael K. Ozanian, "Selective Accounting," *Forbes*, December 14, 1998, p. 124.

ing surfaces, painted on the turf in stadiums or along the boards and under the ice in hockey rinks.

Also not included in the operating revenues that owners are prepared to share equally with players, *Forbes* pointed out, is the money they get for renting luxury boxes at arenas and stadiums, which can amount to tens of millions of dollars every year. The NBA's Chicago Bulls, for example, raked in $12.7 million during the 1997-98 season from the United Center's 216 luxury boxes, but under the league's collective agreement the team only had to declare 40 percent of that figure as income because it was considered ancillary, or only "basketball-related," and not game-related revenue. Most of the $40 million a year paid for the 160 luxury boxes in the Staples Center in Los Angeles, home to the NBA Lakers and NHL Kings, goes not to the teams — and thus not to the players through revenue sharing — but to the office-supplies retail giant the arena was named after, which paid $100 million for the right. Advertising inside the arena, which *Forbes* estimated brings in well over $5 million annually, is similarly diverted to Staples. In short, even as owners were blaming players for refusing to agree to salary caps that would fix their labor costs at a percentage of revenues, according to Ozanian they were fiddling the figures to support their arguments.

It's hard to find much sympathy either for billionaire club owners or for multimillionaire sports stars, but fairness requires us to point out that the owners, in their haste to cry poverty, are taking some liberties with the statistics . . . Spoiled brats many of the players may be, but, hey — they are still entitled to an honest count.[17]

17. Ibid.

Much of the negotiation in subsequent collective bargaining agreements has revolved around increasing the amount of revenue teams share with players. As a result, some of this previously-hidden income has since been included in the NBA's revenue sharing scheme.

FOOTBALL: PROFITING FROM LEAGUETHINK

The NFL has a long tradition of revenue sharing, dating back to the 1930s when the large-market Chicago Bears and New York Giants propped up the small-market Canton Bulldogs and Green Bay Packers. The Bulldogs are long gone, but the Packers are still one of the NFL's powerhouse teams thanks to the league's system of revenue sharing that allows small-market teams to profit from the league's popularity almost as much as clubs in metropolis markets do. According to one textbook on sports economics, this cooperative attitude is the key to the NFL's long-standing success.

> Extensive revenue sharing is the cornerstone of stability of revenues in the NFL . . . Because virtually all NFL teams are privately held, precise figures for revenue sources cannot be determined. More important than the level of revenues, though, is the uniformity created by this extensive system of sharing.[18]

This special brand of socialism for the rich and famous is called "Leaguethink." Over the decades the share-and-share-alike philosophy has come under attack from some of the NFL's most powerful owners, but to this day it remains alive and well. According to most observers it is

18. Leeds and von Allmen, *The Economics of Sports,* pp. 83-84.

responsible for the league's financial prosperity because it "required owners to set aside parochial concerns in the interest of common goals."[19] The *Wall Street Journal* also pointed out that such togetherness has not only led to the league's bottom-line success, but, perhaps not coincidentally, has also resulted in its dominance of the NFL Players' Association. "Leaguethink has kept the NFL largely free from the revenue-labor woes of baseball and hockey, whose clubs divided into Have and Have-Not camps, and led to their current inert states."[20]

While the concept stems from the earliest days of the league in the 1930s, it was kicked into high gear in the 1960s by commissioner Pete Rozelle when he convinced NFL team owners to put him in charge of negotiating a league-wide package of television broadcasting rights with the national networks instead of each team cutting its own deal locally. Those revenues, which have multiplied many times over during the succeeding decades, would then be split equally among all NFL teams under the philosophy, as enunciated by Rozelle, that strengthening the weaker members of the league resulted in a stronger league.

> The basic objective of the league rules is to reverse the process by which the weak teams get weaker and the strong teams get stronger. One sport does not gain on another because of the superiority of their stronger teams. Favorable results are the product of the degree to which each league can stabilize itself through its own competitive balance and leaguewide income potential.[21]

19. John Helyar, "'Leaguethink' links NFL old guarders,'" *Wall Street Journal,* January 6, 1995, p. B10.

20. Ibid.

21. Quoted in Harris, *The League,* p. 14.

The Leaguethink philosophy reached its pinnacle in the mid-1970s, according to NFL historian David Harris, when 95 percent of league revenues were shared, excepting only stadium revenues such as what teams earned from the rental of luxury boxes. A full-frontal attack on the NFL's revenue-sharing cooperative spirit began in 1974 when Oakland Raiders owner Al Davis pulled his franchise out of the league's NFL Properties licensing arm, insisting on being paid directly all the proceeds from the sale of products bearing his team's black and silver logo. Then in a bid to gain more luxury-box revenue that wouldn't have to be shared league-wide, Davis moved his team to a larger stadium with more luxury boxes in Los Angeles in the early 1980s in what Harris described as a "crushing defeat" for Leaguethink.[22] But after a few years in southern California, and after losing a $1.2-billion lawsuit against the NFL, the Raiders returned to the Bay area and Leaguethink resumed its previous cooperative course. In the 1990s it came under attack again by a maverick owner who insisted on profiting from his team's success without having to share the prosperity with on-field rivals. Dallas Cowboys owner Jerry Jones similarly pulled his franchise out of NFL Properties, signing marketing agreements directly with such corporate sponsors as Pepsi and Nike, which resulted in more than a billion dollars worth of lawsuits between the Cowboys and the league.[23]

Obviously not all NFL owners are onside with socialism, but enough are to make it work. And work it does, to the tune of $4.8 million in 2002, according to *Business Week* magazine, which broke down the league's revenues as follows:

22. Harris, *The League,* p. 153.

❖ $200 million (4 percent) from DirecTV's Sunday Ticket, merchandise, NFL Films syndication fees, and sponsorships

❖ $1 billion (22 percent) from local sponsorships, luxury suites, broadcasting, parking, and concessions

❖ $1.1 billion (22 percent) from ticket revenues ($350 million of it is put into a visitors pool and split evenly. Each team gets $10.9 million.)

❖ $2.5 billion (52 percent) from network and cable TV contracts[24]

Of that, only the $1 billion of local revenues — from broadcasting (mostly of pre-season games), luxury boxes, and other stadium revenues — is kept by individual teams. The rest goes into the revenue-sharing pot to be split more or less equally between all thirty-two teams, resulting in 63 percent of total revenues being shared. That amounts to $95.1 million per team in 2002, according to *Business Week*. Of that, a minimum of $72.5 million was shared with players under the NFL's salary cap.[25] Now that is POWERFUL socialism.

HOCKEY: REAP LOCALLY, WEEP GLOBALLY

NHL owners have always been among the most miserly in professional sports when it comes to sharing revenues

23. Jean Jacques Taylor, "Can the NFL Keep Up with the Joneses?" *Sales and Marketing Management*, January 1996, p. 15.

24. Tom Lowry, "The NFL Machine: Behind a Thrilling Season Is a Hard-Nosed Business Run with Military Precision," *Business Week*, January 27, 2003, p. 86.

25. Ibid.

among themselves, not to mention the way they have kept the lion's share from players for decades. According to *Business Week*, the NHL shared only 9 percent of its revenues league-wide in 2002, which was by far the lowest percentage of the four major leagues.[26] (Though as discussed earlier, creative accounting means owners often hide revenues, and share a lower percentage than they have agreed to).

Percentage of Revenues
Major-League Teams Agree to Share

LEAGUE	2002 REVENUES	% SHARED
NFL	$4.8 billion	63
MLB	$3.5 billion	35
NBA	$3.0 billion	34
NHL	$2.0 billion	9

(Source: *Business Week*)

Of course, the NHL's recently expired $50-million deal with ABC was peanuts compared to the network television contracts the other leagues enjoy, so every team has to scramble to make its own deals locally, which they do with greater or lesser degrees of success. Some teams, such as the New York Rangers, are awash in television revenues, while others don't have a television or radio deal at all. It is this disparity in revenues that is proving the NHL's undoing, according to some, and even the league's players' association has included a degree of revenue sharing between teams in its proposal for a luxury tax on payrolls. But if revenue sharing comes to the NHL, what level of transparency could be expected from owners? The busi-

26. Ibid.

ness press has not subjected hockey revenues to the same kind of scrutiny paid to football, basketball, and baseball, but one study suggests that getting straight numbers from NHL owners will take some doing.

When it examined NHL finances in the wake of the ten-day strike by players in the spring of 1992, *Financial World* magazine found not only a wide disparity in revenues between teams, but also much unreported income. One confidential report of league numbers obtained by the business magazine claimed NHL teams lost a total of $25 million on $375 million in revenues during the 1990-91 regular season, and even after playoff revenues were added, they made only a measly profit of $1.2 million. A second report said the league made $46 million profit on $467 million in revenues, including playoffs, that season.

The difference: The healthier numbers include some in-arena revenues. However, both surveys excluded luxury suite revenues other than the ticket value of the seats . . . According to our numbers — and virtually all the teams confirmed the accuracy of FW's estimates of their income statements on a not-for-attribution basis — the league earned $102 million on about $547 million in revenues, a profit margin of 18.7%.[27]

The problem in pinning down the revenues of NHL teams, *Financial World* found, was due to the various levels of cross-ownership, in which some teams, such as the New York Rangers, own their own arenas and even their own broadcasting arms. "Teams with an owner that also owns the arena typically report 'payments' of high

27. Stephen Taub, "Face-Off at the Bottom Line," *Financial World,* July 7, 1992, p. 42.

rent and modest receipts from concessions and other building-generated sources, if any."[28] The Washington Capitals, for example, claimed a loss of $1 million on $20 million in revenues in 1990-91, but those revenues included nothing from arena concession sales and only $25,000 from "special seating," according to *Financial World*. "This obviously refers to its forty skyboxes, which gross about $3 million each year for the 200 or so events in the Capital Centre luxury box sales."[29]

A dozen years later, in the midst of a new round of salary negotiations, NHL owners are again crying poverty, but there are a couple of old adages to bear in mind when listening to their claims. One is about crying wolf, and the other says: "Live by the sword, die by the sword." The NHL spent at least $750,000 to have Arthur Levitt, former chairman of the U.S. Securities and Exchange Commission, supervise an "independent" audit, and his report, released in February 2004, supposedly verified the NHL's claim that its teams lost a combined $273 million during the 2002-03 season. But the players' association viewed the result with caution, claiming that its examination of books from only four teams that it was able to get hold of showed $52 million in unreported revenues.[30]

The one area in which NHL owners have been able to agree on sharing revenues equally among themselves, of course, is expansion fees, which they have been jacking up as high as possible without regard to the long-term

---

28. Ibid.

29. Ibid.

30. Greg Farrell and Adam Shell, "Study Numbers Don't Add Up in Eyes of Players Association," *USA Today,* February 13, 2004, p. C13.

financial viability of the new franchises they allow into the league. As a result, some new entrants have bailed out for less than they paid to get into the league, such as the Atlanta Thrashers, which were basically given away in 2003 as part of the NBA's Atlanta Hawks sale after its original owners paid an $80-million expansion fee to get into the league in 1999. In order to rake in as much in expansion fees as absolutely possible, the NHL board of governors has been issuing new franchises at a dizzying rate since the mid-1990s without regard for the economic consequences. The lessons of the 1970s seem to be lost on them in their quest for a quick buck. Over-expansion during that decade saw teams in Atlanta, Kansas City, Denver, and Cleveland folded or moved. In order to make a short-term killing, NHL owners have demonstrated over and over their willingness to overcook the golden goose.

If Gary Bettman and team owners want to come up with a more workable economic model for the NHL, perhaps they should look beyond simply asking the players to save them from themselves by accepting a salary cap. Maybe they should look at being a little bit less greedy and sharing a bit more among themselves instead — for the good of the game.

CHAPTER 6

Show Me the Money — Salary Disclosure and Arbitration

Over the past decade or so the NHL Players' Association has used salary arbitration and disclosure to ratchet up players' earnings to stratospheric levels (stratospheric for hockey players, at least). Add in some ego economics and a few outright rivalries between owners, and you've got a recipe for wage inflation.

Salary arbitration is a process that was popularized in baseball, where some experts argue it has had a greater inflationary effect than even free agency.[1] Arbitration actually existed in the NHL well before it was introduced to Major League Baseball. Because of the secrecy that surrounded salaries for decades in hockey, however, the process wasn't as effective as in baseball, where there was much more transparency.

Salary disclosure didn't come to the NHL until the 1990s, but since then it has had possibly a greater impact on pushing player contracts upward than salary arbitration has. With the system of transparency set up on Bob Goodenow's watch, every player in the league now knows exactly how much every other player makes.

1. Michael Leeds and Peter von Allmen, *The Economics of Sports* (Boston: Addison-Wesley, 2002), p. 241.

When Alan Eagleson ruled the NHLPA, much secrecy surrounded salaries. Even players on the same team were often unaware of what their teammates were earning. That made it difficult to exert much leverage at contract time, and the secrecy system put most of the bargaining power in the hands of a few big-time agents — such as Eagleson — who had information on the salaries that were being paid to a wide range of players, which he could use at the bargaining table.

Hockey lore abounds with tales from the Dark Ages — before salary disclosure — of players blissfully unaware of what others were earning and playing for peanuts as a result. The classic involves Mr. Hockey — Gordie Howe — and is recounted by David Cruise and Alison Griffiths in their 1991 book *Net Worth*, which revealed many of the shady business practices used for decades by NHL owners, aided and abetted by their pal Al at the players' association. Howe, a gentle giant off the ice who turned all elbows once on skates, led the NHL in scoring six times (the first four times in consecutive seasons from 1950-51 to 1953-54, by an average of eighteen points) and placed among the top five for a phenomenal twenty straight seasons. But at contract time, Mr. Hockey was, in contrast to his on-ice demeanor, a bit of a pushover.

Taking advantage of Howe's trusting nature, Detroit Red Wings general manager Jack Adams offered to let his star player fill in his own salary each year before signing a new contract, and the modest Prairie product would usually award himself a paltry $1,000 raise. Howe played in the era before agents did the negotiating for players, which was pioneered in the mid-1960s by Eagleson on behalf of Bobby Orr. That development led to the first big step up in salaries for NHL players, but by 1968

Howe was still earning just $45,000 after nineteen years in the league. When defenceman Bob Baun was traded to Detroit in 1968, according to Cruise and Griffiths, he set Howe straight in no uncertain terms about how little he was making and how much he had held hockey salaries back as a result.

> "You've held us back for ten years and perhaps longer," he told a surprised Howe. "Some of the older fellows would probably say you held the league back twenty-five years" . . . When Baun revealed his own $67,000 annual contract, the great number 9 simply gaped in amazement . . . "If you thought more of yourself, you'd get what you're worth. Why don't you try, this year, filling in $150,000 and see what he does," challenged Baun.[2]

When an angry Howe filled in his contract for 1969, according to Cruise and Griffiths, he demanded $100,000, to which Red Wings owner Bruce Norris grudgingly agreed. What neither Baun nor Howe knew at the time was that Detroit had just signed defenceman Carl Brewer for $126,000, and that the Red Wings had recorded a profit of at least $1 million annually on hockey operations since 1946, plus another $1 million or so running the Olympia arena.[3] The NHL franchise in hockey-mad Detroit had for decades been one of the most profitable operations in all of professional sports, unbeknownst to the Red Wings players because NHL owners annually

2. David Cruise and Alison Griffiths, *Net Worth: Exploding the Myths of Pro Hockey* (Toronto: Penguin, 1991), p. 8.
  3. Ibid., p. 9.

cried poverty and implored them to settle for lower salaries "for the good of the game."

How things have changed in the thirty-five years since Mr. Hockey had his revelation. Howe retired shortly thereafter, but he unretired a few years later to play in the WHA with his sons, Mark and Marty. Finally he got to make the big bucks, which he was so justly entitled to after so many years of exploitation. When the NHL and WHA merged in 1979, Howe was still playing, and he suited up for the last time in professional hockey that season at the age of fifty-three.

Even then only the tip of the iceberg was showing in the NHL's financial shell game, and it took some investigative reporting by such journalists as Cruise and Griffiths, along with Russ Conway and Bruce Dowbiggin, to get to the bottom of the league's pyramid of duplicity. By the time their work was done, Eagleson had been sentenced to eighteen months in prison for fraud and was ordered to pay CDN$1 million in restitution to retired NHL players, but some players complained that Eagleson got off lightly by cutting a deal in Canada instead of being sentenced in the U.S., where he had also been charged and where the justice system is nowhere near as forgiving. He was out on parole within six months and also escaped having to face a multi-million-dollar class-action lawsuit brought in the U.S. by several former NHL players in 1998. The players sued Eagleson and the NHL for conspiracy, claiming that up to US$50 million had been wrongly diverted from the NHLPA pension fund. A judge in Philadelphia, however, threw the lawsuit out in 2001 because by the time it was launched the four-year statute of limitations for racketeering had long passed since the first reports of Eagleson's malfeasance surfaced in *Sports Illustrated* in 1984, and even since they were chronicled in detail in *Net Worth* in 1991.[4]

Now that the players finally have the upper hand at the bargaining table, the league is again crying poverty and asking them to take less "for the good of the game." It's no wonder the NHLPA is skeptical. Given their past experience with NHL team owners, hockey players can be excused for doubting the numbers trumpeted by the league in making its case for insolvency. To borrow the famous catchphrase of Tom Cruise as sports agent Jerry Maguire in the movie of the same name, they say, "Show me the money." Financial transparency isn't a lot to ask, but it's the only thing that's worked for professional athletes so far. Here's how.

SALARY ARBITRATION

The 1973 collective bargaining agreement in Major League Baseball introduced the concept of salary arbitration to America's pastime, and the first cases were decided the following year. By then the MLB Players' Association was clamoring for free agency following the unsuccessful court challenge it had financed on behalf of Curt Flood. Team owners agreed to some half measures in response, such as allowing veteran players to veto a trade, and allowing unresolved salary disputes to be settled by arbitration if the player had been in the major leagues for at least two seasons. It was through the arbitration process that baseball players finally won the right to free

---

4. Mary Ormsby, "U.S. Court Upholds NHL Ruling — Former Players Waited Too Long to Sue Alan Eagleson," *Toronto Star*, June 26, 2001, p. E6.

agency, but most of the subsequent salary increases in Major League Baseball have come through the arbitration of salaries for players who have not yet put in enough years of service to qualify for free agency.

Baseball players had tried for decades to get salary arbitration, but it was only when an increasing number of individual players "held out," refusing to show up for spring training — or opening day — in support of their contract demands, that they finally convinced Major League Baseball owners to agree to an arbitration system to settle salary disputes. Even then, some owners were opposed to arbitration because they foresaw the inflationary effect it would have on salaries. "We'll be the nation's biggest assholes if we do this," warned Oakland A's owner Charles O. Finley, who also owned the NHL Seals, a 1967 expansion team that relocated to Cleveland as the Barons in 1976 before being merged with the old Minnesota North Stars (now the Dallas Stars) in 1977. "You'll have a system that drives up the average salary every year. Give them anything they want, but don't give them arbitration."[5]

Arbitration is a science in and of itself, and is practiced by specialists. Most of them are lawyers, but some are former labor negotiators or other professionals experienced in bargaining. Arbitration is a "quasi-judicial" process that is based on a few fundamental principles and then follows a system of "precedent," similar to what judges use to decide court cases in the legal system. The process has been used for many years to resolve disputes in busi-

5. Kenneth M. Jennings, *Swings and Misses: Moribund Labor Relations in Professional Baseball* (Westport, CT: Praeger, 1997), p. 40.

ness and in collective bargaining, most commonly to settle a strike or lockout, by having an impartial third party
look at the matter and decide on a fair settlement. When
they take their dispute to arbitration, the two sides basically agree to disagree on the issues, at the same time
agreeing on the need for both sides to get back to work.

An arbitrated settlement can either be *binding,* which
means both sides have to agree in advance to accept it, or
non-binding, in which case the dispute starts all over
again if one or both sides don't agree with the arbitrator's
decision. But even binding arbitration can involve a lot
of game-playing on both sides, with negotiators making
unrealistic demands in anticipation of an arbitrator split-
ting the difference and awarding a settlement somewhere
in the middle. To avoid this problem and force the sides
to be realistic, a process of *final offer arbitration* is often
used, and this is the system that was introduced to
decide salaries in MLB. Each side presents an offer to the
arbitrator and then makes its best argument for why it
should be accepted instead of the other side's. A half-day
hearing is held, and written arguments are commonly
submitted as well. The player signs two contracts before
the hearing starts — one for the salary offered by the
club, and another for the salary he is seeking. After hearing arguments from both sides, the arbitrator then
decides which contract to tear up and which one should
be registered with the league.

In baseball, submissions are made during the off-season, from January 15 to 25, and hearings are held from
February 1 to 20. Arbitrators generally issue their deci-
sions within twenty-four hours and are not required to
provide written reasons for choosing one side's number
over the other. Only one-year contracts can be signed

under the arbitration process in MLB, but even after an arbitrator's ruling is made, the sides can agree on a multi-year contract for a different salary. After its first two decades of use, there had been 376 salary arbitration hearings in baseball, and the cumulative score stood at 210-166 in favor of management.[6]

Increasingly, baseball players and their agents have filed for arbitration as a bargaining tactic in hopes of gaining some leverage with which to negotiate a higher salary without actually having to go all the way to an arbitration hearing. In the first five years of MLB salary arbitration, more than 43 percent of players who filed for arbitration ended up going to a hearing — with the rest settling their contracts before then — but by the 1990s that percentage had dropped drastically. The number of filings increased three- or fourfold from the 1980s to the 1990s, but the percentage going all the way to a hearing dropped into the teens. Of course, even players who "lost" their salary arbitration cases ended up as big winners financially, with salary increases averaging greater than 50 percent annually — some years as high as 95 percent on average, as in 1990. Players who won their arbitration cases almost always had their salary more than doubled, with increases ranging as high as 174 percent on average in 1984 and 1993.[7] Proving Charlie O's prophecy prescient, arbitration has proven a driving force behind the wildly escalating salary structure in baseball over the three decades since its introduction.

6. Paul D. Staudohar, *Playing for Dollars: Labor Relations and the Sports Business,* 3rd ed. (Ithaca: Cornell University Press, 1996), p. 41.

7. Jennings, *Swings and Misses,* p. 43.

From less than $41,000 on average in 1974, salaries have increased to an average of $2.5 million in 2004.

One of the more bizarre results of salary arbitration in baseball is its reliance on ever more arcane statistics. Arbitrators rely almost entirely on objective criteria, because subjective player qualities, such as leadership abilities, are difficult to put a dollar value on. Thus, intangibles don't count for much in the numerical equation used to determine player salaries under the arbitration system. This has created a growth industry in obscure statistical categories in a sport that was already a statistician's wildest dream. An arbitrator is now faced with such statistics as "strike zone judgment" and "inherited runner percentage" in determining a pitcher's worth. He or she (yes, some arbitrators are women) is then asked to make sense of this statistical stew in order to issue an award for either the team or the player. The high-stakes number crunching has taken advantage of a whole new science called "sabermetrics," a term coined in the late 1970s that refers to the Society of American Baseball Research, or SABR, to which many of the figure filberts belong.[8] Computerized averages of accomplishment and correlations of efficiency are crunched annually at arbitration time in an attempt to demonstrate a player's value — or lack thereof.

Expert players in the "rotisserie league" of baseball — named after the New York restaurant where the big league of fantasy competition was founded in 1980 — have turned pro in the high-stakes game of salary arbitration. Bill James, author of many a statistical abstract in

8. Richard Rapaport, "Stats All, Folks," *Forbes,* April 11, 1994, p. 62.

baseball, now charges hundreds of dollars an hour for adding his numerical expertise to a player's case and even attends arbitration hearings to spout statistics that will back up arguments made by agents. Teams have jumped on the stats bandwagon in self-defence, developing sophisticated computer programs to support their own arguments for keeping arbitration awards down.[9]

THE NHL EXPERIENCE

Salary arbitration in hockey predates its introduction in baseball by five years. The NHLPA got the league to agree in 1969 to a process in which salaries could be decided by arbitration if the player and team — and, of course, the player's agent — couldn't agree on a contract at the bargaining table. The original process was cumbersome and ineffective, and thus seldom used before the advent of salary disclosure, and without detailed information on what other players were earning, it appears to have had little effect on NHL salaries.

Under the first rules for salary arbitration in the NHL, both the league and the NHLPA named one arbitrator apiece, and the two of them together considered the case. If they couldn't agree on a salary, they named a third arbitrator, who made a binding decision. Unlike in baseball, salary arbitration in the NHL does not restrict the arbitrator(s) to choosing between the final offers of each side, which makes the process considerably more complicated. In 1971 the system was modified to name a single arbitrator, Edward J. Houston, to hear all salary arbitrations in the NHL. The single-arbitrator system was officially incorpo-

9. Ibid.

rated into the 1975 collective agreement, which named Gary E. Schreider as the arbitrator for salary disputes.[10]

Not much is known about NHL salary arbitrations in the 1970s and 1980s, as salaries were kept secret by agreement between the league and the NHLPA. One textbook on collective bargaining in baseball attempted in 1981 to compare the salary arbitration systems in the two sports, but the author proved unable to do so. "The lack of salary data prevents us from presenting any empirical estimates as to the impacts of the availability of salary arbitration in hockey," wrote Professor James Dworkin of Purdue University. "Hopefully this issue will be addressed in the near future by someone well-trained in scientific inquiry."[11] Unfortunately for hockey fans, most labor relations scholars appear to be much more interested in baseball, which has seen numerous studies of the impact of free agency and arbitration on salaries. Many fewer must be hockey fans, or perhaps it's a result of the lack of published data, as Professor Dworkin suggests, because no scholarly studies of salary arbitration in hockey have yet resulted. There are two organizations that do keep very close track of salary arbitrations in hockey nowadays, but they don't publish their data, nor their conclusions. They are the National Hockey League and the NHLPA, both of which have sophisticated computer programs to analyze statistical categories, player salaries, and arbitration awards.

During the Dark Ages of NHL salary secrecy, the *Hockey News* and other newspapers occasionally got hold of a

10. James B. Dworkin, *Owners versus Players: Baseball and Collective Bargaining* (Boston: Auburn House, 1981), pp. 264-265.

11. Ibid., pp. 263-264.

copy of the super-secret NHL salary list and published it, as the Toronto *Globe and Mail* did in 1978. Its listing of every NHL player's pay showed that Phil Esposito, then playing out the end of his career with the New York Rangers, was the league's salary champion at $325,000, followed closely by Marcel Dionne of the L.A. Kings at $320,000. The newspaper's figures, which it said were obtained through a "survey of agents and NHL executives," showed that many players were making less than $50,000, including rookie winger Dave Taylor of Los Angeles, who earned only $45,000. Most teams did not have a player earning more than $150,000, and the highest-paid player on the Washington Capitals' roster was listed as Guy Charron, at $85,000.[12]

The NHL immediately denied the accuracy of the *Globe and Mail*'s numbers, but the cat was out of the salary bag in more ways than one that week in 1978.[13] Two of the WHA's biggest stars jumped to the NHL as free agents, with the New York Rangers signing undrafted Swedes Ulf Nilsson and Anders Hedberg to contracts worth $725,000 in salary, with a signing bonus of $225,000 each.[14] The big-money signings had NHLPA boss Alan Eagleson in an uproar in the same issue of the *Globe and Mail* that listed NHL salaries. "I thought that over the past five or six months we were getting to the point where common sense was a little more prevalent in hockey at the man-

12. "Who Makes What in the NHL," Toronto *Globe and Mail*, March 14, 1978, p. 37.

13. "NHL Executive Disputes Globe List of Salaries Paid to Hockey Players," Toronto *Globe and Mail*, March 15, 1978, p. 33.

14. Bruce Dowbiggin, *Money Players: How Hockey's Greatest Stars Beat the NHL at its Own Game* (Toronto: McClelland & Stewart, 2003), p. 52.

agement level," muttered the Eagle, noting that the NHLPA had gone easy on the league in recent negotiations after the NHL claimed it was losing millions annually. "Our position now will be: 'If you've got $2 million for two hockey players maybe you've got a couple of hundred thousand for some more pensions.'"[15] Still, few realized the Eagle was firmly in the pocket of NHL president John Ziegler, who groused in response that such sabre-rattling by the NHLPA boss concerned owners, who were attempting to restore "economic sanity" to the game.

The WHA soon collapsed completely, leaving hockey players with no bargaining power whatsoever. While NHL salaries had more than quadrupled in the 1970s, from an average of $25,000 in 1970 to $108,000 by 1980, they did not even double over the following decade and scarcely kept up with inflation, reaching only $211,000 by 1990.[16] Unlike the situation in baseball, where salaries increased more than eightfold in the first decade of salary arbitration — with a little help from free agency, of course — the few salary arbitrations heard in the NHL obviously had little impact on hockey salaries, to answer Professor Dworkin's question as best we can. All that changed after NHL players voted to finally make their salaries public in late 1989.

15. Donald Ramsay, "Sittler, McDonald May Want Pay Hikes," Toronto *Globe and Mail,* March 14, 1978, p. 37.

16. The U.S. Consumer Price Index — the traditional measure of inflation — rose 57 percent from 1980 to 1990, while NHL salaries climbed 95 percent on average, meaning the "real" increase in the average NHL salary during the 1980s was only 38 percent, in contrast to 223 percent during the 1970s, after deducting 109 percent for price inflation (salary figures from Leeds and von Allmen, *The Economics of Sports,* p. 226).

SALARY DISCLOSURE

An important concept in labor relations was identified by Clark Kerr, the former president of the University of California, who coined the term "orbits of coercive comparison." It's a fancy name for a common-sense proposition — that workers will demand to be paid as much as others whose work they consider to be of comparable value. And they will probably go on strike if they aren't being paid at least as much as those whose efforts they consider to be of lesser worth. The concept has been used for decades by union negotiators in formulating wage demands and gaining the solidarity of their union members to hold out for what they think they're worth. Different unions, in turn, use settlements in other industries for purposes of "coercive comparison" to argue for higher increases, and the result tends to be an unending cycle of wage escalation. The same concept applies in white-collar jobs as well, where workers will similarly formulate their own salary demands — and adjust their output of effort — according to what their colleagues are being paid. This is known in management research as "equity theory," and it also applies to the executive ranks. CEO's salaries have risen recently, often into the multi-million-dollar range depending on the success of their companies — and on how much other CEOs are paid. The cycle of escalation can only work, however, if wages and salaries are disclosed, as they usually are in union contracts and company reports.

The disclosure of NHL salaries had been resisted for decades by key elements in the NHLPA, notably Eagleson and some of his clients who held top positions on the executive committee of the players' association and benefited in their own contract settlements from the Eagle's greater access to salary information. Yet as the 1980s drew to a close, a series of uprisings against Eagleson's rule of the NHLPA led to a growing sense of militancy within the ranks of players. In the summer of 1989, Eagleson was forced to hire an assistant who would eventually take over leadership of the NHLPA. That fall the issue of salary disclosure was finally put to a vote.

A few of Eagleson's cronies warned against disclosure. "It puts players in an awkward position," argued NHLPA president Bryan Trottier. "It could create tax problems." Bobby Smith, whose Montreal Canadiens voted against salary disclosure, attributed it to "the kind of feeling that no information is better than the wrong information. And there was a question of privacy. Guys don't want to see it as open as it is in baseball, where all the salaries are printed in the papers."[17] But by 1989 a feeling was growing among NHL players that they had been left behind in the salary bonanza of the 1980s, which had seen pay raises in all the other pro sports that were double what hockey players had received. Many players pointed the finger at Eagleson, and some wondered why their union chief was playing not just both sides of the table, but multiple roles as agent, union head, international hockey organizer, and even landlord of the NHLPA offices in Toronto.

When salary disclosure passed overwhelmingly by a vote of 469-49,[18] Eagleson claimed he had been in favor of the idea all along, and it had been the players who opposed it. "As recently as 1988-89, 25 percent only were

17. Alan Adams, "NHL Players Vote for Salary Disclosure," *Edmonton Journal,* November 25, 1989, p. H2.
18. Ibid.

in favor of salary disclosure," he told CBC television reporter Bruce Dowbiggin.[19] But the players tell a different story. "For every player against it, there were ten for it, maybe more," veteran forward Pat Verbeek told newspaper reporter Russ Conway.[20] "Eagleson kept telling us it wouldn't help us," added goaltender Andy Moog.[21]

The effect of salary disclosure in the NHL was pronounced and immediate. While there were only two players — Wayne Gretzky and Mario Lemieux — making $1 million or more annually before salary disclosure, within two years the ranks of the NHL "Millionaires Club" had swollen to sixteen. "The players have enjoyed incredible salary increases without having applied so much as superficial pressure," mused *Toronto Star* hockey writer Bob McKenzie. "What's going to happen when they really start turning the screws?"[22]

The wage escalation between 1989 and 1991 was boosted, of course, by the St. Louis Blues' big-money signings of Brett Hull and Scott Stevens in the summer of 1990. After earning $125,000 the previous season with the Blues, Hull got a new contract worth $7.3 million over three years as a restricted free agent. Stevens was handed $5.1 million over four years to jump from the Washington Capitals, with whom he had been earning $300,000. Besides demonstrating the magnitude of money available to free agents despite the draconian compensation rules in place, the significance of the sign-

19. Quoted in Russ Conway, *Game Misconduct: Alan Eagleson and the Corruption of Hockey* (Toronto: Macfarlane Walter & Ross, 1995), p. 161.

20. Ibid.

21. Ibid., p. 162.

22. Bob McKenzie, "Hockey Salaries Going Up, Up, Up," *Toronto Star,* October 31, 1991, p. B1.

ings was that they showed just how the escalation process could benefit from the insecurities and egos of owners. Once the Blues started shelling out the megabucks, other owners and general managers followed suit in an attempt to keep up. It was as if a dam had burst, and the rising water level carried every salary negotiation upward with it. At the time, Chicago Blackhawks general manager Bob Pulford observed that the salary escalation in the first years of salary disclosure may have been started by St. Louis, but it was continued in every other NHL city. "As Pogo says, 'We have identified the enemy and it is us,'" said Pulford. "The enemy is not the players' association or the players. Those of us in management in the National Hockey League are the people paying them all that money. Nobody is forcing us to do it."[23]

The rules as written in the collective agreement hadn't changed, only the way the game was played by the NHLPA had, thanks to salary disclosure. Coercive comparison allowed every player negotiating a contract to point to the salary made by every other player in the league and say "I want that." Or more. As Bob McKenzie noted in 1991, owners and general managers could have said "no" to the big money demands.

No to Kevin Stevens. No to John Cullen. No to Luc Robitaille. No, no, no, a thousand times no. The rules haven't changed, have they? Being a free agent in the NHL is just as restrictive now as it was three years ago, right? In fact, NHL owners have reacted nervously and poorly to the Blues' big moves.[24]

23. Mike Kiley, "NHL on Crash Course with Spiralling Salaries," *Ottawa Citizen,* October 24, 1990, p. C3.
24. McKenzie, "Hockey Salaries Going Up, Up, Up."

The classic example of using the new-found bargaining leverage was Brett Hull's contract, which one agent described as "an education in negotiation" conducted by his agent, a Harvard-trained lawyer named Bob Goodenow. "He hung on, he used all the levers, and he used them well," marveled the unnamed agent of Goodenow's bargaining tactics. "He's a *very* ballsy guy."[25] It was a sign of things to come from Goodenow on behalf of the NHLPA. By 1991 the number of million-dollar players in the NHL more than doubled, to thirty-three, led by rookie Eric Lindros at $3.5 million.[26] The average NHL salary had also more than doubled in the previous four years.

It was Bob Goodenow who was hired in 1989 as assistant executive director of the NHLPA, to apprentice as Eagleson's replacement. Goodenow had represented numerous NHL players over the years as an agent. According to Cruise and Griffiths, he had also been "deeply involved" in the long-running revolt against Eagleson, which began with an attempted coup by several player agents in 1986, although Goodenow managed not only to keep his name out of the paper trail, but also to play both sides of the fence so successfully that "both factions came away convinced he was on their side."[27] Goodenow, whom the *Net Worth* authors describe as "inscrutable," went about bringing a change in bargaining tactics to the players' association as he bided his time "with the sublime patience of a heron stalking fish" while Eagleson threw roadblocks in his way. In 1991 Bob

25. Cruise and Griffiths, *Net Worth*, p. 371.

26. "Millionaires Far More Prominent in NHL," *Calgary Herald*, September 22, 1992, p. D5.

27. Cruise and Griffiths, *Net Worth*, p. 338.

28. McKenzie, "Hockey salaries going up, up, up."

McKenzie reported that the Eagle's assistant was putting in place a "comprehensive plan" to maintain the upward pressure on salaries through full disclosure and a "complete overhaul" of the arbitration process.[28]

Eagleson was scheduled to depart in early 1992,[29] but by the time the collective agreement expired on September 15, 1991, his world was collapsing as first the investigative reporters, and then the authorities, caught up with him. Goodenow was soon free to bring his brave new world of collective bargaining to the NHLPA.

Salary disclosure was one of the prime weapons in the arsenal Goodenow unleashed against owners. It also included the ultimate weapon, which he detonated by taking the players out on strike as the 1992 playoffs approached. NHL president John Ziegler and team owners hardly knew what hit them, according to Cruise and Griffiths, and were totally taken aback by the switch from dealing with the winking, pliable Eagleson to the hardline tactics of the unreadable Goodenow.

Eagleson's modus operandi of entering negotiations unprepared and weaponless, with few staff, few experts, no research, no consensus among members, no strike fund and no strike vote, was discarded with breathtaking speed once Bob Goodenow unpacked his briefcase in Toronto in the summer of 1990.[30]

The scene was set for the lockout of 1994.

29. Cruise and Griffiths, *Net Worth,* p. 372.
30. Ibid., p. 368.

ESCALATION BY ARBITRATION

The new agreement that was signed after half the 1994-95 season had been canceled by the owner-imposed lockout contained changes to free agency that they hoped would help stem the tide of salary increases. It also put some restrictions on salary arbitration for restricted free agents, such as limiting the season for hearings to August 1 to 15. According to reporter Bruce Dowbiggin, this forced player agents and the NHLPA to find new ways to hike salaries, and that's when "the arbitration game commenced in earnest."[31] With Goodenow's guidance, and his assistant Ian Pulver's ingenuity, the NHLPA devised a system for both preparing arbitration cases and arranging them in order of presentation for their best chances of success. The players whose cases were backed up with the strongest scoring statistics would go to arbitration first in hopes of winning lucrative awards that could be used in turn as precedents for arguing the cases of lower-scoring players.

Unlike in baseball, many valuable qualities of hockey players are difficult to quantify with statistics, but even the dullest general manager realizes the importance of defensive play, toughness, and leadership ability in players. Given their tendency to rely on scoring statistics, arbitrators tended to hand out big awards to players who lit up the scoreboard despite having none of the aforementioned intangibles. NHL teams did have the right under the collective agreement to walk away from arbitration awards they considered unreasonable, but in doing so they forfeited their rights to that player, who

31. Dowbiggin, *Money Players*, p. 220.

then became a free agent without compensation. That amounted to such a considerable personnel loss, however, that it rarely happened in NHL salary arbitrations. When it did happen, such as in 1999 when the Boston Bruins renounced their rights to forward Dmitri Khristich, who was awarded $2.8 million by an arbitrator, the player was often able to sign for an even higher salary with another team eager to add to its personnel without having to give up compensation. Khristich ended up signing a four-year contract with the Toronto Maple Leafs at an average salary of $5 million — almost double the arbitrator's award.

In the late 1990s the NHL began to develop a more extensive system of statistics (in an attempt to attract figure filberts as fans) and also added several new awards — such as the Bud Light Trophy for the best "plus-minus" rating.[32] The league soon found these being used as weapons against it in salary arbitrations. Agents built their arguments for greater salary awards to players on the newly created categories — such as blocked shots, "hits," and faceoff-winning percentages. In an attempt to prevent this tactic, the NHL decided to stop keeping some of these statistics in 2002. The NHLPA filed a grievance against the decision. The players' association argued that these categories had become part of the arbitration process and couldn't be removed without its agreement. An arbitrator sided with the players and ordered the statistical categories restored in 2003.[33]

32. A player's "plus-minus" rating refers to the difference between the number of even-strength goals scored by his team while he is on the ice, whether or not he scored or assisted on the goal, and the number scored against his team while he is playing.

33. Dowbiggin, *Money Players*, p. 216.

As a result of working these levers of salary arbitration, the NHLPA has been able to increase player salaries almost continually since salary disclosure was introduced in 1990. NHL team owners are desperate to change the system, and if they can't get rid of salary arbitration altogether — as would be their preference — they would at least like to take the decision on the order in which players come up for their hearings out of the hands of the NHLPA.

Just how serious the league is about changing the economic landscape by forcing this sort of cost-saving change on players will determine how long NHL play will be suspended by a lockout. But playing hardball in labor negotiations can backfire if the power relations turn out to be not quite as anticipated. If the NHL gambles big and cancels its 2004-05 season, it could lead to the end of the league as we know it.

CHAPTER 7

CBA '04–'05 —
The Ultimate
Power Play

The collective bargaining relationship is based on power. The amount of power held by each side in labor negotiations influences its bargaining position, and the strength of its position in turn determines how favorable a settlement it can obtain. But the ultimate resolution of any labor dispute is not simply a result of power dynamics. If it was, we could feed the variables into a computer that would spit out the settlement terms, and everybody could get back to work.

Instead, of course, collective bargaining outcomes are also affected by a variety of intangible factors, such as the strategy and tactics of the negotiators, and the skill and cunning with which each side "sells" its position to the other — and to the public. Labor-management relations are a fluid, dynamic process in which things can change quickly — and unexpectedly — once push comes to shove at the bargaining table and on the picket line. They are also a long-term relationship, in which each side must be careful not to beat up the other guy so badly that he holds a grudge for the next scheduled rematch.

Each side in negotiations will have worked up every imaginable scenario in order to prepare for the unexpected turn of events and also to come up with a few curveballs to throw the other bargaining team. By examining the respective advantages of each side, and by factoring the known variables into the equation, we can come up with a general idea of how long the impasse in negotiations between the National Hockey League and its players' association might last. But the unexpected — by definition — is difficult to predict. For a student of labor relations, a good old-fashioned bargaining-table dustup ranks right up there with a fracas between two tough guys at a hockey game.

If you listen to the public pronouncements made by both sides, and if you believe the press reports on progress of the 2004 NHL contract talks, the inescapable conclusion is that the opposing camps are deeply entrenched and that a protracted deadlock is inevitable. After all, both sides have been rattling sabres for several years now — and not just along the boards in Buffalo. However, if you take with a grain of salt what the point men for each side say and discount it as probably posturing, you have a better chance of answering the question of how long the dispute might go on. By focusing on what each side has to gain — and to lose — we can come up with some clues as to what is going on behind closed doors and get a better idea of the likely outcome. More importantly, we can try to figure out when the talking might finally stop and the puck might finally drop.

THE CREDIBILITY GAP

One of the NHL's biggest problems as it attempts to force concessions from the NHLPA on such things as free agency and salary restraints is that despite the league's best efforts to paint a picture of poverty, the players aren't buying it. They've heard that line before, they believed it when it wasn't true, and as a result, for many years NHLers earned by far the lowest salaries of major-league athletes. As far as they're concerned, the past decade has been "payback time" for all those years the owners pulled the wool over their eyes at contract time. Now that they've caught up to and passed the average salary paid to players in the National Football League — even though they trail their contemporaries in basket-ball and baseball by a wide margin — NHL players are reluctant to give back their hard-won gains. They want to keep the limited free market system as it is, and they point out that nobody forces owners to pay inflated salaries for free agents.

The NHL has trotted out its high-priced financial expert in the form of Arthur Levitt to attest to the fact that the league really is losing money by the bushel, as it claims. The players are understandably skeptical and have challenged the league to open its account books to the NHLPA's scrutiny rather than simply pay someone hundreds of thousands of dollars to vouch for its honesty. Some pundits point to the fact that it was under Levitt's stewardship of the U.S. Securities and Exchange Commis-sion from 1993 until 2001 that "cooking" the account books of giant corporations reached its height, when the accounting boondoggles at Enron, Worldcom, and a host of others were taking place. In an attempt to bolster its claims of financial ruin and narrow its cavernous credi-bility gap, the NHL could have chosen a more reputable spokesman.

Hockey players to a man are repeating the mantra of Cuba Gooding Jr. and Tom Cruise in the movie *Jerry Maguire* — "Show me the money" — which has been adopted by every professional athlete fortunate enough to be playing today. However, NHL players also seem to understand that the capacity of owners to pay increasingly higher salaries may have already been reached, or even exceeded, especially with the league's guaranteed television revenues petering out as its contract with ABC expires. Some high-profile puck chasers, such as Brett Hull and Jeremy Roenick, have gone on the record as saying that the vast majority of NHL players are overpaid, and the NHLPA kicked off collective bargaining for a new agreement at the start of the 2003-04 season by offering to take a 5 percent salary rollback across the board and agree to a luxury tax on payrolls if owners agreed to redistribute the tax proceeds to small-market teams as a form of revenue sharing. That wouldn't fly with Bettman, however, who reportedly wants a hard salary cap of $31 million per team — which is calculated to be low enough to guarantee a profit for owners based on current revenues.

WAGING THE WAR OF WORDS

Perhaps the best weapon that NHL owners have for pressuring players to accept a new collective bargaining agreement that contains provisions for "cost certainty" is the one that has best served this purpose in the past — influencing public opinion through the media. By portraying players as greedy and overpaid and appealing publicly to them to settle for less "for the good of the game," team owners have always been able to gain the high ground in the court of public opinion and influence the average hockey fan against the NHLPA. By blaming players for high ticket prices or for the shutdown of the game during labor disruptions — even if it is the owners themselves who have locked the doors to the ice rinks — the NHL has managed to gain sympathy in the press.

After all, the sports reporters who cover the games — and the labor disputes, despite frequently being unqualified to explain the issues — are dependent on team management for their very press passes.

At least, that's the way it always played out when Alan Eagleson was in the game. Since the Eagle landed in jail and Bob Goodenow began looking after the best interests of players, though, the NHL has had an image problem. Thanks to the investigative reporting of a few journalists with expertise in the business side of sports, who have helped expose the league's exploitation of players over the decades, the tables have turned to a certain extent.

Some courageous reporters who are less beholden to owners have even turned the spotlight on their own colleagues in the press and asked why they served so long as toadies for management. Russ Conway, of the aptly named *Eagle-Tribune* in Lawrence, Massachusetts, did much of the investigative work that led to Eagleson's downfall and found some interesting connections that helped explain his masterful manipulation of the media. Not only was Eagleson chummy with sportswriters in every NHL city, which helped him receive favorable press coverage for his stewardship of the NHLPA, but according to Conway he greased a few palms as well. Former *Toronto Sun* sports editor George Gross reportedly got a $10,000 interest-free loan from one of Eagleson's clients, along with tennis tickets to Wimbledon. Longtime Montreal *Gazette* sports editor Red Fisher, according to Conway, was also a shareholder in Bobby Orr Enterprises, a company Eagleson had set up to invest the earnings of his best-known client but which turned out to be a losing proposition. When the bottom fell out of Orr's investments, Fisher received a generous $15,000 payout nonetheless, according to Conway.

On two occasions, I asked Fisher about the $15,000. He seemed startled that I knew about the deal and refused to talk. I wanted to ask him how a sports reporter can remain objective when he has financial ties to the people he's writing about. Fisher is a long-time supporter of Eagleson; his newspaper . . . has given remarkably little coverage to Eagleson's past practices and legal woes.[1]

Former CBC television reporter Bruce Dowbiggin also noticed the Eagle's media machine, in which "key reporters in each city became his de facto PR agents." Eagleson's failure to win free agency for NHL players at the bargaining table got little press coverage from reporters who "never said a critical word about Eagleson's achievements."[2] Not only did Eagleson fail to win many concessions from management on behalf of players, noted Dowbiggin, but he even helped NHL owners unify themselves in bargaining against the players' association by mediating disputes between some of the most fractious members. "The spoon-fed media rarely pointed any of this out, of course, preferring to deify the man who'd always been good for a bottle of scotch at Christmas and a scoop on mundane hockey matters."[3]

Not all hockey writers kowtow to management. Some try to walk an independent course without being unduly influenced by either side, and some are actually on the side of the players. A few are openly antagonistic to man-

1. Russ Conway, *Game Misconduct: Alan Eagleson and the Corruption of Hockey* (Toronto: Macfarlane Walter & Ross, 1995), p. 251.

2. Bruce Dowbiggin, *Money Players: How Hockey's Greatest Stars Beat the NHL at Its Own Game* (Toronto: McClelland & Stewart, 2003), p. 47.

3. Ibid., p. 54.

agement and have been threatened with revocation of their press passes and banishment from NHL arenas. Sports talk-show hosts whose commentary is deemed insufficiently favorable to local team management may find they are unable to arrange for guests to appear on their programs.

Like all daily press reporters, hockey writers are measured by the quality and quantity of "scoops" they can provide for their newspaper's pages. Thus they tend to rely on a few trustworthy sources to obtain their information, which often comes conveniently through either team management or, on the other side, player agents. By tracking where a reporter gets his inside information, readers may easily divine that journalist's loyalties. Other more obvious clues can be found in the nature of the copy filed, without even reading between the lines. Many agents have enlisted the aid of journalists to influence public opinion as they negotiate contracts on behalf of their clients. One example would be the case of Pavel Bure, who was described by Vancouver *Province* columnist Tony Gallagher as "Mr. Underpaid" during his contract dispute with the Vancouver Canucks. Gallagher's penchant for taking the side of players in salary negotiations has hardly endeared him to team management, but it has ensured that he's first in line for hockey scoops leaked by cagey agents to sympathetic journalists.

Writers who dig a bit deeper than the daily press usually does often emerge with a vastly different perspective than what is conveyed by most sportswriters. Economists who study compensation theory tend to categorize professional athletes as entertainers, who contract with promoters to share their special talents, rather than as workers who simply sell the sweat of their toil. As a result, those economists have come to the conclusion that professional athletes are actually underpaid in light of the revenues they bring to team owners. Scholars in fields that are more concerned with questions of social justice tend to see the relationship between team owners and their players as one of exploitation, as David Mills notes.

> Popular literature and sports journalism . . . with few exceptions, tend to portray team owners as folk heroes. But serious academic works by sports economists, historians, and sociologists often evoke an equally simple image — the team owners as robber baron.[4]

The truth probably lies somewhere between the two extremes. Whether fans see NHL players as spoiled and overpaid or as noble and exploited depends on their own prejudices, which can be manipulated by the "spin" provided by the public relations experts employed by either side in the dispute. As a result, public perceptions about who is to blame for putting NHL games on hold will depend more on public relations than on the facts, such as who locked the doors to the ice rinks.

MANIPULATING THE MEDIA

The secret to manipulating public opinion, according to Walter Lippmann, the writer who coined the term, lies in restricting the public's access to information. By emphasizing selected points that bolster a position and ignoring those that don't, not to mention disseminating misinfor-

---

4. David Mills, "The Blue Line and the Bottom Line: Entrepreneurs and the Business of Hockey in Canada, 1927-90," in *The Business of Professional Sports*, eds. Paul D. Staudohar and James A. Mangan (Urbana, IL: University of Chicago Press, 1991), p. 38.

mation through the press, public opinion can thus be influenced in favor of one side or the other. Lippmann was a journalist, not an academic, and he noticed this phenomenon after he was drafted into the U.S. publicity effort during World War I. By depicting the Germans as vicious, baby-killing Huns, the hastily formed Committee on Public Information was able to turn American sentiment against Germany in short order. The Committee used graphic imagery in a poster campaign and in the new medium of Hollywood movies, and a nation that for the first two years of the Great War had been staunchly isolationist suddenly became rabidly interventionist. The art of public relations had been born, and over the years it has developed into a sublimely subtle science that is often worked to perfection by its practitioners.

The secret of public relations, Lippman wrote, was in the difference between the pictures in people's heads and the actual state of affairs — what he called "the world outside."[5] A PR expert uses stereotypes, misinformation, and even disinformation to create a picture that is considerably different from reality. Presenting professional athletes as greedy, overpaid villains who are holding out for more money would influence public opinion against NHL players, but it would ignore the fact that it is team owners who have shut down the game. The skillful use of select information and powerful imagery is key to the public relations battle that will doubtless be fought during the current labor dispute, as it was in the NHL's previous shutdowns.

During the dispute that resulted in the ten-day player's strike in 1992, according to the authors of *Net Worth,*

5. Walter Lippmann, *Public Opinion* (New York: Macmillan, 1922), p. 1.

then-president John Ziegler was well-coached in presenting the league as a beleaguered guardian of the great game of hockey. According to Cruise and Griffiths, Ziegler's "hundreds of hours of laborious work with his media guru Bill Wilkerson finally paid off" when he was able to use the media to portray players as "selfish, ungrateful and callous."[6] Ziegler claimed in interviews that NHL teams would lose a collective $150 million in the next three years if the league gave in to player demands. He shed tears in one masterful performance on *Hockey Night in Canada,* noted Dowbiggin, sniffling: "I don't know if our fans will ever forgive us."[7] The only problem, according to Dowbiggin, was that Ziegler was using "ridiculously inflated" figures in media interviews.

A particularly effective ploy in the NHL owners' repertoire was the constant repetition of the fact that the NHL players' average salary was $379,000. After the strike, League general counsel, Gil Stein, admitted that the real figure was $233,900.[8]

The fact that NHL teams had together racked up $150 million in profits over the previous three years was conveniently forgotten, noted Cruise and Griffiths, as was the fact that the owners had recently taken in another $150 million in expansion fees from aspiring franchise holders. Unfortunately for the NHL, this blatant deception backfired on them when NHLPA members voted

6. David Cruise and Alison Griffiths, *Net Worth: Exploding the Myths of Pro Hockey* (Toronto: Penguin, 1991), p. 376.

7. Dowbiggin, *Money Players,* p. 134.

8. Cruise and Griffiths, *Net Worth,* p. 376.

560-4 to strike after "the owners' tactics radicalized the players in a way that Bob Goodenow could never have hoped to do by himself."[9]

Stein, who briefly held the post of NHL president after Ziegler stepped down following the 1992 strike, perhaps proved too honest to serve as head of the league and was replaced by Bettman. Stein admitted later in his memoirs that, for years, collective bargaining sessions with the NHLPA under Eagleson had largely been "staged" for the benefit of the players and public, with the Eagle actually agreeing to a final settlement days earlier over drinks with Ziegler and team owners.[10] In the Brave New World of salary disclosure under Goodenow, there can be no fudging of the facts as far as player salaries go, but team finances are still significantly less than transparent, which leaves as an open question the owners' honesty in pleading poverty. In light of their past experience with the league, NHL players are understandably sticking to their mantra: Show me the money.

According to long-time New York hockey writer Stan Fischler, Gary Bettman began his publicity campaign for the 2004 collective bargaining negotiations in 1999, shortly after the league extended the deal to allow NHL players to participate in the Olympics.[11] Since then, according to the commissioner, the agreement negotiated in 1994 — and extended twice at the league's behest — has gone from being one that would save the game of hockey from greedy players to one that will prove its ultimate ruin if not changed. And who is the culprit, as usual? Not spend-

9. Ibid., p. 377.

10. Quoted in Dowbiggin, *Money Players,* p. 56.

11. Stan Fischler, *Cracked Ice: An Insider's Look at the NHL* (Lincolnwood, IL: Master's Press, 1999), p. 304.

thrift owners, but overpaid, greedy players. The question is: How many will believe it again? The answer will determine just how strong the NHL's bargaining position will be as it plays hardball with its players.

THE FRUITS OF THEIR LABORS

One clue to how long the NHL shutdown might last can be found in labor economics. Research has found that the more people are paid, the less they want to — or have to — work. Those who are paid low wages or salaries will usually work as much overtime as they can get because they need the money. This is known as the "substitution effect," and it means that lower-paid workers gladly substitute leisure time for more income. The flip side of this coin is called the "income effect," under which those who earn very high wages or salaries will gladly work less in exchange for more leisure time. In professional sports, this phenomenon can be seen in the case of such players as former NBA star Michael Jordan, who walked away from a multi-million-dollar salary in 1997 by "retiring." After a season of working on his golf game, Jordan was back in uniform for the Chicago Bulls. As one textbook on sports economics noted: "The extraordinary level of income that Jordan generated early in his career allows him the option of working very little or not at all."[12]

The same high salaries that NHL owners are trying to get rolled back in collective bargaining with their players are what will allow the players to hold out for a long time in support of the status quo. When the league began threatening a shutdown of play in the long lead-up to

12. Michael Leeds and Peter von Allmen, *The Economics of Sports* (Boston: Addison-Wesley, 2002), p. 228.

negotiations, Goodenow advised the players to start squirreling some money away to enable them to stand firm. As the Vancouver *Province*'s Tony Gallagher pointed out, not only are today's high-paid NHLers better positioned financially to hold out during a lockout, but some of the veteran players must be "almost dancing with joy" for the opportunity to take time off. With many players now playing into their forties in the talent-diluted NHL, older veterans would welcome the opportunity to give their bodies a rest from the grueling NHL schedule in which most playoff teams play over a hundred games a year, including exhibitions.

> Imagine a month in Hawaii during the winter, a first-time experience. Imagine being at home, taking the kids to and from school every day for a couple of semesters. The only reason they have any concern is because a lot of other people they know and meet every day at the rink will be out of work. So they will be concerned and will try to avoid a lockout. But financial pressure? Are you joking?[13]

Not only that, but there are income opportunities for players besides the NHL, such as playing in Europe or the reconstituted WHA, and the longer the shutdown continues, the more opportunities are likely to be available in response to demand from hockey-starved fans. The 1994-95 lockout, perhaps not coincidentally, was settled shortly after players announced plans to form their own ten-team league and play a thirty-game schedule. Revenues

13. Tony Gallagher, "No Pressure on Players: With Bags of Money Already in Hand, They Can Afford a Lockout," Vancouver *Province*, January 25, 2004, p. A78.

from the NHLPA league would have been distributed among all members of the players' association, not just those who suited up for games. The proposed league planned to place teams in cities with large arenas that were not controlled by NHL teams, such as the 17,000-seat Copps Coliseum in Hamilton or Vancouver's city-owned Pacific Coliseum, where the Canucks played for twenty-five years before building their own arena. The players' league even reportedly negotiated a television deal with the CTV network that called for nationally televised double-headers on Saturday night in the long-standing tradition of CBC's *Hockey Night in Canada*.[14]

IN THE CONTRACT ZONE

Now that the NHL's pendulum of power has finally swung in the favor of players over the past decade or so, their reluctance to loosen their grasp on it is understandable in light of past experience. They like things the way they are because, unexpectedly, the 1995 collective agreement has turned out very much in their favor, financially. It's the league that has provoked this latest labor dispute in a bid to lower its costs of doing business and swing things back its way. One way to do that is by influencing public opinion, but that only sets the stage for the nitty-gritty, down-and-dirty work that has to be done at the bargaining table. The NHL has provided the impression for five years or so that it is willing to shut the game down if players won't give in. Whether it is bluffing or not is less important than whether players believe it.

14. David Shoalts, "League of Their Own — Union Planning Its Own Games," Toronto *Globe and Mail,* January 10, 1995, p. D8.

Labor relations theory holds that for a collective bargaining agreement to be negotiated, the range of outcomes acceptable to management and labor must overlap in what's called a "contract zone." Somewhere within this zone, depending on the skill of the negotiators and resolve of the stakeholders, a settlement can theoretically be achieved. If the settlement ranges of the two sides don't overlap — as apparently is the case in talks between the NHL and NHLPA — then a strike or lockout is inevitable. The strike or lockout will go on until the ranges of acceptable settlements move to meet at a settlement point. Striking or locked-out workers start getting hungry (or bored) and become more willing to go back to work for less than they were originally demanding — sometimes even for less than they were originally making if management is insisting on concessions or a wage rollback. Similarly, owners begin to miss out on revenue and may see new competitors, such as rival leagues, start up to take their customers away, so they become more willing as time goes on to settle with their workers and get back to business. Several models have been developed over the years in an attempt to predict union and management behavior in labor negotiations. The two main kinds of bargaining models are economic and behavioral.

Economic bargaining models basically assume that both sides act rationally and in their own financial self-interest, whether that be in the short-term or the long-term. Either side might be willing to endure short-term losses — such as missed paychecks or lost ticket sales — in exchange for winning concessions from the other side that will bring about a long-term improvement in its financial fortunes. The basic tradeoff under this model is short-term pain for long-term gain, and the length of a strike or lockout will basically depend on how well-prepared each side is to hold out in support of its demands. If workers or players have built up a strike fund from their union dues, out of which they can pay themselves enough to cover at least their living expenses, they can afford to hold out for a long time. Similarly, if business owners have lots of money in the bank — or strike insurance, if they can get it — they can hold out against the demands of a union or in support of their own demands for wage reductions, or whatever.

Most economic bargaining models take a cost-benefit analysis approach to determine how long each side should be willing to endure a strike or lockout (its cost) in return for winning a better settlement (its benefit). Calculating the benefit — or "utility" in economic terms — of each side in a labor dispute is not enough, however. Because it takes two to tango at the bargaining table, the "joint utility" of the two sides together must be analyzed in order to calculate at what point they maximize their benefits. That's because some items may be in the interest of both sides to share — the classic "win-win" situation — while others may be benefits that can only be distributed to one side — a "win-lose" item. For example, agreeing to increase the number of games played should result in a benefit to both owners and players, as each side would make more money. Lowering the percentage of revenue to be shared by owners with players, however, would reduce salaries and thus benefit only the owners.

Behavioral collective bargaining models have more to do with psychology than with money, and they commonly focus on relations between the negotiators for each side and on the internal politics of each constituency. Sometimes during contract talks, rational economics go out the window and negotiations become a matter of ego and machismo, like children fighting in a schoolyard. The animosity that builds up across the bargaining table and the posturing that goes on both before and during talks can make it difficult for either side to give in without losing face — and credibility. The personalities of the chief negotiators may clash, and the negotiators may also have to deal with union executive and ultimately the rank-and-file membership or, in the case of Gary Bettman, the thirty NHL team owners. Typically in labor negotiations, management has an advantage by being more united because only one owner or a small group of owners is involved, and often it can employ "divide and conquer" tactics by appealing to the interests of only a portion of union members. But when thirty strong-willed, ego-driven owners are involved, the "cat-herding" a negotiator like Bettman must do to keep them all together on the issues can be more taxing than the negotiations across the table. No doubt that's exactly why the NHL commissioner has insisted on the extraordinary powers granted him by owners in order to take a hard line with the players.

Finally, because the union-management relationship is usually a long-term one, influencing and structuring the attitudes of the other side is an important tactic. One side might not want to take advantage of the other too badly at the bargaining table if it suffers a temporary weakness, for fear of the other side seeking revenge the next time around and attempting to set things right by forcing a prolonged work stoppage. But if a fundamental change in the collective bargaining agreement is required due to a growing imbalance in the power relationship, it is wise for the side seeking the change to give long and loud notice of its intention. That's no doubt exactly what Bettman and the NHL owners have been doing with the dire warnings they have issued over the past several years. This way, at least, everybody knows what's coming, and the players can think long and hard about exactly how strongly they want to resist the push by owners for a salary cap. Public posturing in such a high-profile dispute inevitably influences the eventual compromise reached, and this can be worth millions in the end.

Mathematician John Nash, that quirky Nobel laureate played by Russell Crowe in the movie *A Beautiful Mind,* came up with an interesting economic bargaining model in 1950. His model dealt with labor negotiations, such as those in the NHL, when you have what's called a "bilateral monopoly" — that is, a single employer of labor on one side and a single seller of labor, a union, on the other. One of the model's central findings was that a group's bargaining power in such a case stems from its ability to walk away from the bargaining table and pursue outside opportunities of value. Nash called this a side's "threat point." The higher either side's threat point is, the more bargaining power it has. What are the alternatives NHL owners have to reaching an agreement with the NHLPA? Hiring replacement players, inducing players to scab, staging circuses, or switching to lacrosse. The players? Why there's Europe, the WHA, forming their own barnstorming teams and possibly even their own league, etc. According to Nash's model, the "threat point" enjoyed by the players in this case is obviously higher than that of the owners, so the players have more bargaining power and should have the advantage in a standoff, as their alternatives are more attractive than those facing the owners.

MEDIATION AND ARBITRATION

Sometimes the two sides across the bargaining table get so dug in, and their hopes of agreeing on a settlement become so bleak, that nothing can get them out of the hole they find themselves in except some outside help. That's when a couple of processes long used in labor relations can prove beneficial.

The first is *mediation,* under which an outsider is brought in to help the sides find some common ground by better defining the issues, outlining the consequences of failing to find a settlement, and hopefully bringing the sides close enough together to reach a compromise. Both sides have to agree on a mediator, and he or she must be of sufficient stature to influence the outcome. U.S. president Bill Clinton attempted to mediate in the 1995 Major League Baseball strike after the shutdown extended from one season to the next, even bringing the negotiators for each side to the White House for talks. Clinton appointed an outside mediator to recommend a solution to the base-ball impasse and proposed that the matter go before Congress for a resolution if the sides still could not agree. Congress was reluctant to become involved, however, and eventually the players and owners came to an agreement on their own.

But who would have sufficient stature to mediate the NHL labor dispute? It is, after all, an international disagreement. How about the World Court?

If mediation doesn't bring about a settlement, the sides can go to *arbitration* — the same process used to settle salary disputes in the NHL and MLB. Often when talks get fractious, both sides agree to arbitration as a face-saving way out of their stalemate. Sometimes some level of government steps in to impose a settlement in the public interest, but hockey is entertainment and could hardly be considered an essential service.

But who could arbitrate the labor dispute in the NHL? The NHL operates across borders, so under applicable labor laws neither the Canadian or U.S. government can claim jurisdiction over the sport. Mediation or arbitration would have to be a voluntary process agreed to by both the NHL and the NHLPA, and neither side would likely get to that stage of desperation until at least one season has been canceled. And by then, who knows? The landscape of hockey may have changed so much that a new agreement is superfluous. If NHL owners decide to play hardball in collective bargaining by shutting down the world's top hockey league indefinitely, they could soon find themselves rendered redundant by simple laws of economics.

RINK BRINKSMANSHIP

A settlement of the NHL labor dispute is not likely to come soon after September 15, 2004, the long-dreaded expiry date of the previous agreement. That six-year deal, the result of the four-month shutdown of the league in 1994-95, was twice extended at the NHL's behest in exchange for labor peace during the league's rapid expansion of the late 1990s and also to allow the participation of NHL players in the 1998 and 2002 Winter Olympics. But now the price that will have to be paid to establish economic balance has increased several times over. The players like the league's economics just the way they are, and they have been preparing for several years now to hold out against the owners' demands for change.

At the same time, even the most hard-headed puck chasers have to admit that not only have they never had it better, financially, but their prosperity could turn out to be a fragile thing if they push their luck too far. The NHL's dire economic straits took a turn for the worse just as the 2004 Stanley Cup playoffs were heating up, when the league announced a new national television contract with NBC. The deal contains no revenue guarantees for the league, instead promising . . . wait for it . . . revenue sharing from the broadcasts. The only guaranteed national television money the NHL has to look forward to is the $60 million or so it gets from cable giant ESPN.[15]

Some more outspoken hockey stars freely admit that they are overpaid, and the NHLPA's October 2003 offer to take a wage rollback of 5 percent reflects an acceptance of that reality. How much farther than that they might be willing to go, however, remains to be seen. Don't expect Bob Goodenow to cave in early to the demands of Gary Bettman and NHL owners for major concessions on free agency or a salary cap. According to Dowbiggin, Goodenow well understands that almost all labor disputes are settled at the last minute, under the high-stakes deadline pressure of brinkmanship, earning him the nickname "Eleventh-Hour."[16] The last time push came to shove between the NHL and its players in 1994, it took until mid-January before a last-minute compromise was reached in order to save the season. Even then, the league didn't get the salary restrictions it claimed

15. Stefan Fatsis, "NHL Scores 0 for TV Rights in NBC Deal," *Wall Street Journal,* May 19, 2004, p. B1.

16. Dowbiggin, *Money Players,* p. 123.

were needed to save the game. Its plight in the ensuing decade has only worsened, making it likely that the NHL will indeed follow through on its threats to cancel the entire 2004-05 season to get its way.

Who will blink first? What if neither side blinks? That scenario could see a total reshaping of the hockey landscape.

THE DEATH OF THE NHL?

Hockey is on the brink. Of what, it's hard to tell. One doomsday scenario goes like this: A prolonged suspension of NHL play results in a migration of hockey talent overseas to play in Europe, as was seen on a limited scale in 1994. This time the lockout lasts much longer, and the excess supply of hockey talent leads to the creation of a European "Super League" that expands across national boundaries throughout the EU by taking on idled hockey stars, both European and North American. This would effectively reverse the "brawn drain" that has taken place over the past two decades, with players migrating in large numbers from European leagues to play in the world's top league in North America. With the NHL closed for business in the event of a labor dispute, however, the door would be opened for a shift of the center of hockey supremacy from hockey-mad Canada to hockey-mad Europe. Worldwide broadcast revenues from North American television networks like TSN, ESPN, and even the CBC would doubtless be forthcoming with a shortage of hockey programming back home and fans there clamoring to see their favorite players on their new teams. This would allow the European teams to pay top salaries to attract star players, which would lessen the incentive for players to settle their dispute with the NHL and, in the event of a prolonged shutdown, create the possibility of the European league's expansion into North American markets, creating a true World Hockey Association and the death of the NHL. Couldn't happen, you say?

Hmmmmmmmmmm . . .

Bibliography

Badenhausen, Kurt, Cecily Fluke, Lesley Kump, and Michael K. Ozanian. "Double Play; Why a Moneylosing Baseball Team Is Worth $700 Million." *Forbes,* April 15, 2002, p. 92.

Conway, Russ. *Game Misconduct: Alan Eagleson and the Corruption of Hockey.* Toronto: Macfarlane Walter & Ross, 1995.

Cruise, David, and Alison Griffiths. *Net Worth: Exploding the Myths of Pro Hockey.* Toronto: Penguin, 1991.

Dowbiggin, Bruce. *Money Players: How Hockey's Greatest Stars Beat the NHL at Its Own Game.* Toronto: McClelland & Stewart, 2003.

Dworkin, James B. *Owners versus Players: Baseball and Collective Bargaining.* Boston: Auburn House, 1981.

Fischler, Stan. *Cracked Ice: An Insider's Look at the NHL.* Lincolnwood, IL: Master's Press, 1999.

Harris, David. *The League: The Rise and Decline of the NFL.* New York: Bantam Books, 1986.

Holzman, Morey, and Joseph Nieforth. *Deceptions and Double-cross: How the NHL Conquered Hockey.* Toronto: Dundurn, 2002.

Jay, Paul. "How Open Books Saved the NBA." *Profit,* March 2004, pp. S16-S18.

Jenish, D'Arcy. *The Stanley Cup: A Hundred Years of Hockey at Its Best.* Toronto: McClelland & Stewart, 2001.

Jennings, Kenneth M. *Swings and Misses: Moribund Labor Relations in Professional Baseball.* Westport, CT: Praeger, 1997.

Jones, J.C.H., and William D. Walsh. "Salary Determination in the National Hockey League: The Effects of Skills, Franchise Characteristics, and Discrimination." *Industrial and Labor Relations Review,* July 1988, pp. 592-604.

Kesenne, Stefan. "The Impact of Salary Caps in Professional Team Sports." *Scottish Journal of Political Economy,* September 2000, pp. 422-430.

Leap, Terry L. *Collective Bargaining and Labor Relations.* New York: Macmillan, 1991.

Leeds, Michael, and Peter von Allmen. *The Economics of Sports.* Boston: Addison-Wesley, 2002.

Levitt, Arthur Jr. *Independent Review of the Combined Results of the National Hockey League 2002-2003 Season.* (Westport, CT: Arthur Levitt Jr., 2004.

Lippmann, Walter. *Public Opinion.* (New York: Macmillan, 1922.

Lowry, Tom. "The NFL Machine: Behind a Thrilling Season Is a Hard-Nosed Business Run with Military Precision." *Business Week,* January 27, 2003, pp. 86-94.

McKelvey, G. Richard. *For It's One, Two, Three, Four Strikes You're Out at the Owners' Ball Game.* Jefferson, NC: McFarland, 2001.

McKinley, Michael. *Putting a Roof on Winter: Hockey's Rise From Sport to Spectacle.* Vancouver: Greystone, 2000.

Miller, Marvin. *A Whole Different Ball Game: The Sport and Business of Baseball.* Secaucus, NJ: Carol, 1991.

Noll, Roger G., ed. *The Government and the Sport Business.* Washington: Brookings, 1974.

Ozanian, Michael K. "Selective Accounting: Most team owners claim to be losing money. Depends on how you count." *Forbes,* December 14, 1998, pp. 124-129.

———. "Inside Pitch: How Baseball Team Owners Dupe the League's Revenue-Sharing System." *Forbes,* April 28, 2003, p. 64.

Ozanian, Michael K., and Brooke Grabarek. "Foul!" *Financial World,* September 1994, p. 18.

Papanek, John, and Bill Brubaker. "The Man Who Rules Hockey." *Sports Illustrated,* July 2, 1984, pp. 62-74.

Parker, Dan. "The Hockey Rebellion." *Sports Illustrated,* October 29, 1957, pp. 19-21, 67.

Quirk , James, and Rodney D. Fort. *Pay Dirt: The Business of Professional Team Sports*. Princeton, NJ: Princeton University Press, 1992.

Rapaport, Richard. "Stats All, Folks." *Forbes,* April 11, 1994, pp. 62-69.

Scully, Gerald W. *The Market Structure of Sports*. Chicago: University of Chicago Press, 1995.

Staudohar, Paul D. "The Football Strike of 1987: The Question of Free Agency." *Monthly Labor Review,* August 1988, pp. 26-31.

—-. *Playing for Dollars: Labor Relations and the Sports Business,* 3rd edition. Ithaca: Cornell University Press, 1996.

———. "Salary Caps in Professional Team Sports." *Compensation and Working Conditions,* Spring 1998, pp. 3-11.

———. "Baseball Negotiations: A New Agreement." *Monthly Labor Review,* December 2002, pp. 15-22.

Staudohar, Paul D., and James A. Mangan, eds. *The Business of Professional Sports*. Urbana, IL: University of Chicago Press, 1991.

Szymnski, Stefan; and Stefan Kesenne. "Competitive Balance and Gate Revenue Sharing in Team Sports." *Journal of Industrial Economics,* March 2004, pp. 165-177.

Taub, Stephen. "Face-Off at the Bottom Line." *Financial World,* July 7, 1992, p. 42.

Taylor, Jean Jacques. "Can the NFL Keep Up with the Joneses?" *Sales and Marketing Management,* January 1996, p. 15.

Vrooman, John. "The Economics of American Sports Leagues." *Scottish Journal of Political Economy,* September 2000, pp. 364-398.

Walker, James R. "Time Out: Viewing Gratifications and Reactions to the 1987 NFL Players' Strike." *Journal of Broadcasting & Electronic Media,* Summer 1990, pp. 335-350.

Walton, Richard E., and Robert B. McKersie. *A Behavioral Theory of Labor Negotiations: An Analysis of a Social Interaction System*. New York: McGraw-Hill, 1965.

Index